2019-20
101 WAYS TO
SAVE
MONEY
ON YOUR TAX
LEGALLY!

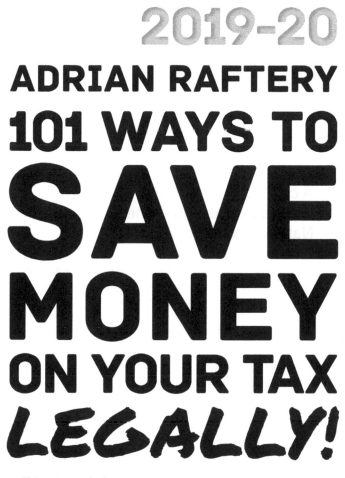

2019-20

ADRIAN RAFTERY

101 WAYS TO

SAVE MONEY

ON YOUR TAX

LEGALLY!

THE ESSENTIAL GUIDE FOR ALL AUSTRALIAN TAXPAYERS

WILEY

CONTENTS

PART VI

YOUR SUPERANNUATION 147

⚠ PITFALL

When you see this box throughout the book, it will outline a potential pitfall in relation to this money-saving strategy that you need to look out for.

🎁 BONUS RESOURCES

When you see this box throughout the book, it will provide you with a tool or a calculator available on my website www.mrtaxman.com.au to help explain or work out a strategy.

? FAQ

When you see this box throughout the book, it will provide you with an answer to a frequently asked question that I have received from readers of previous editions of this book.

📢 PROPOSED CHANGE

When you see this box throughout the book, it will outline a tax change which has been proposed by the government but has not been put through as legislation as at date of publication. Before making any decisions, ensure that you check the status of these proposed changes as there may be variations to the original proposal as it passes through both houses of parliament.

INTRODUCTION

Six years ago, my wife and I were extremely fortunate to celebrate the birth of our son Hamish via a friend who acted as a surrogate mum. Before we started the surrogacy process, I remember her telling us that she had a gift to bear children, but 'a gift is not a gift unless it is given'.

I feel the same way about this book. Ever since I started working as an accountant at the age of 18, I have had a gift (some would say it is a curse) for understanding tax. But as a gift should be given, I have decided to share some great tax tips with you for a small tax-deductible fee (that is, the price of this very cheap book!).

This book has two objectives. First, I would like to help maximise everyone's refunds by making you more aware of the different ways that are available to help you save money on your tax legally. Second, through the setting of boundaries, I wish to reduce the amount of fraudulent claims made so that we all pay a fairer share of tax.

My motivation for writing this book was the number of families out there who didn't understand all the different types of government benefits and tax concessions that were available to them. I hope that this book will help reduce the confusion and that you will start claiming more of what you are legally entitled to.

This book is split into various parts in line with some key areas surrounding your finances:

- you and your family
- your employment
- your education
- your investment property
- your shares
- your superannuation
- your business.

1 MARRIAGE

Accountants are frequently asked two questions by couples who are just about to get married: 'Are there any tax implications once we tie the knot?' and 'Do we need to start doing joint tax returns?'

Your wedding day is a special day. So I'm perplexed as to why on earth the bride and groom are thinking about the ATO during such an exciting time in their lives!

You don't need to worry about tax in the lead-up to your nuptials. Unless you are involved in a business together, you don't have to lodge a combined tax return. Any share of joint investments, such as interest, dividends and rental properties, is still recorded separately in your respective tax returns.

> ♀ **TIP**
>
> You don't have to lodge a combined tax return if you're married. Any joint income is recorded separately in your respective tax returns.

You do need to show on your return that you now have a spouse, and disclose his or her taxable income each year.

> ⚠ **PITFALL**
>
> The combined income of married couples is taken into account if you don't have private health insurance (an extra 1 per cent Medicare levy is charged if you earn over $180 000 combined, increasing to 1.5 per cent for couples earning more than $280 000) as well as when calculating Family Assistance Office benefits such as child care rebates and family tax benefits.

If you elect to change your name, you can notify the tax office:

* by phone on 13 28 61
* by post after completing the *Change of details of individuals form* (NAT 2817)

- or online via your MyGov account at www.my.gov.au. Make sure it is linked to the ATO.

You will need either your Australian full birth certificate; your Australian marriage certificate; or your Australian change of name certificate.

According to the ATO, the definition of spouse has been extended so that both de facto relationships and registered relationships are now recognised. Your 'spouse' is another person (whether of the same sex or opposite sex) who:

- is in a relationship with you and is registered under a prescribed state or territory law
- although not legally married to you, lives with you on a genuine domestic basis in a relationship as a couple.

♦ TAX FACT

Since 1 July 2009, people living in same-sex relationships have been treated in the same way as heterosexual couples for tax purposes. The ATO has outlined some of the tax concessions now open to same-sex couples, including:

- Medicare levy reduction or exemption
- Medicare levy surcharge
- dependant (invalid and carer) tax offset
- senior and pensioner tax offset
- spouse super contributions tax offset
- main residence exemption for capital gains tax.

It is not unusual to find a couple where each owns a main residence that was acquired before they met. However, spouses are only entitled to one main residence exemption for capital gains tax (CGT) purposes between them. If both members of a couple own a main residence they must do either of the following:

- select one residence for the exemption
- apportion the CGT exemption between the two residences.

Provided the homes meet the requirements for the main residence exemption, they will both be wholly exempt from CGT for the period prior to the couple being treated as spouses. However, from the time the couple became spouses, only one exemption is available, though this may be divided between the two dwellings.

> ✎ **EXAMPLE**
>
> Mary bought a house in 1992. She lived in it right up to the day she married Matthew in 2006 and moved into his house, which he had purchased in 2000. As they elected to treat Matthew's house as their main residence, Mary will be subject to CGT on her house from 2006. She will not be liable for CGT on any capital growth in the 14 years prior to becoming Matthew's spouse.

2 INCOME SPLITTING

Income splitting is a legitimate tax-planning tool and one of the easiest strategies to implement. There are a few simple strategies for you to follow and they all mainly revolve around the marginal tax rates for yourself and your spouse, both now and in the future. The tax rates for individuals, not including the Medicare and other levies, are shown in table 1.1.

The goal is to try to level the income of couples so that they are paying tax at the same marginal rate. While income from personal exertion (such as your salary) cannot be transferred to the other partner, there is scope to have passive income from investments transferred if the assets are held in the lower-earning spouse's name.

TABLE 1.1: tax rates for individuals excluding levies (2019–20)

Taxable income	Tax on this income
0–$18 200	Nil
$18 201–$37 000	19c for each $1 over $18 200
$37 001–$90 000	$3572 plus 32.5c for each $1 over $37 000
$90 001–$180 000	$20 797 plus 37c for each $1 over $90 000
$180 001 and over	$54 097 plus 45c for each $1 over $180 000

Source: © Australian Taxation Office for the Commonwealth of Australia.

It amazes me how many smart business people are really dumb when it comes to reducing tax. Too often I see rich business people paying the highest tax rate (47 per cent including medicare levy) on interest or dividend income while their spouses don't fully use their $18 200 tax-free threshold. With a $1.6 million transfer balance cap on superannuation that came into effect 1 July 2017, there is an opportunity to split superannuation contributions between spouses such that each spouse maximises their respective $1.6 million thresholds before they retire.

♀ TIP

Ensure that all investments are in the name of the lower-earning spouse so that they can take advantage of the lower tax rates (particularly the first $18 200, which is tax-free) on any investment income derived. Likewise, have all passive deductions, such as charitable donations, in the higher-earning spouse's name as they may get a return of up to 47 per cent, depending on their income level.

The best tax outcome can be achieved with a low-income earner holding investment assets. They could earn up to $21 884 tax-free (see p. 15), receive a refund of all imputation credits and pay less tax on capital gains.

✎ EXAMPLE

If an investor on the top marginal tax rate of 47 per cent had a $100 000 capital gain they would pay $23 500 in tax and Medicare levy. If an investor with no other income had a $100 000 capital gain they would pay $7467 — a saving of $16 033.

⚠ PITFALL

Any tax benefit derived by transferring an income-producing asset from one spouse to another may be lost if there is CGT to pay on assets originally acquired after 19 September 1985.

If you transfer an income-producing asset to your spouse you may need to find out the market value of the asset from a professional valuer. This is regardless of what you actually receive because the transaction is not independent nor is it at arm's length. In this situation either party could exercise influence or control over the other in connection with the transaction.

3 DEPENDANT (INVALID AND CARER) TAX OFFSET

The dependant (invalid and carer) tax offset (DICTO) is only available to taxpayers who maintain a dependant who is genuinely unable to work due to carer obligation or disability.

- your adjusted taxable income as the primary income earner was $100 000 or less
- your dependant's adjusted taxable income was less than $11 150
- you and your dependant were Australian residents (not just visiting).

If you satisfy the above and your dependant's adjusted taxable income was $285 or less and you maintained him or her for the whole year, you can claim the maximum dependant (invalid and carer) tax offset of $2717.

⚠ PITFALL

The DICTO is reduced by $1 for every $4 that your dependant's adjusted taxable income exceeds $282.

♀ TIP

You may be able to receive more than one amount of DICTO if you contributed to the maintenance of more than one dependant during the year, including if you had different spouses during the year.

♠ TAX FACT

The ATO defines your 'adjusted taxable income' as the sum of the following amounts, less any child support that you have paid:

- taxable income
- adjusted fringe benefits
- tax-free pensions or benefits
- income from overseas not reported in your tax return
- reportable super contributions
- total net investment loss for both financial investments and rental properties.

4 CHILDREN

Any income that has been earned by your child's efforts, such as wages from an after-school job, is considered 'excepted income' and is taxed at the general adult tax rates regardless of whether your child is under 18. However, you should be cautious when putting investments in your child's name because minors do not enjoy the same tax-free thresholds as adults on this type of income, known as 'eligible income'. Table 1.2 sets out the tax rates that apply to minors' eligible income.

TABLE 1.2: tax on eligible income for minors (2019–20)

Taxable income	Tax on this income
$0–$416	Nil
$417–$1307	66c for each $1 over $416
$1307 and over	45% of total income

Source: © Australian Taxation Office for the Commonwealth of Australia.

⚠ PITFALL

Minors under the age of 18 are taxed at the highest marginal tax rate for 'eligible income' (such as interest, dividends and trust distributions) over $416 per annum.

If some of your child's income is excepted income and the rest is eligible income, they will pay ordinary rates on the excepted income and pay at the higher rate on the eligible income.

✏ EXAMPLE

Louie is 17 on 30 June. He earned $8780 from a part-time job. He also received $920 in interest from money he had saved over the years from gifts. Therefore, he has an excepted income of $8780 and is entitled to the tax-free threshold of $18 200 for this income. He also has eligible income of $920 interest, which is taxed at the special higher rates.

A child is eligible from birth for a TFN from the ATO. If your child is under 16 (at the start of the calendar year) and does not supply their TFN to the bank or share registry, then 45 per cent tax will be withheld on interest earnings over a threshold of $420 as well as on all unfranked dividends. If your child is aged 16 and over, then the threshold is reduced to $120.

Children do not need to lodge a tax return if their assessable income is less than $416. However, if tax has been withheld from them by an investment body or employer, then they must lodge a return in order to get that money returned to them.

♀ TIP

If you have an adult child who has a job while going to university or TAFE then they may be able to claim a deduction for certain expenses if there is a sufficient connection between their course and their assessable income. Some expenses that they might be able to claim in this instance include:

- depreciation of assets (such as computers, desks and bookshelves) used for studying purposes
- journals and periodicals
- photocopying and printing costs
- stationery
- textbooks
- travel from work to place of study.

They wouldn't be entitled to a deduction for any tuition fees payable under HELP or any repayments of outstanding HELP debts.

Earnings from a child's investments must be declared by the person who rightfully owns and controls the investment, not the person whose name it is in, or whose name it is held in trust for. This is regardless of whether the money is spent on resources for the child.

> ### ✏ EXAMPLE
>
> Sarah opens an account for her three-year-old daughter, Samantha, by depositing $8000. Sarah is signatory to the account and she also makes regular deposits and withdrawals to pay for Samantha's preschool expenses. The ATO would deem that the money belongs to Sarah and any interest earned from this account must be declared for tax by her.

If the funds in the account are made up of money received as birthday or Christmas presents, pocket money or savings from part-time earnings such as newspaper rounds, and these funds are not used by any person other than the child, then the interest earned is the child's income.

> ### ⚠ PITFALL
>
> Children are not eligible for the low-income tax offset against unearned income, such as interest. The rebate can only be offset against excepted income.

5 PAYMENTS FOR NEW PARENTS

There are a few government payments available when becoming a mum or a dad.

Paid parental leave

Eligible working parents of children born or adopted may be entitled to the paid parental leave scheme to help them care for a new baby. The pay is for up to 18 weeks at the national minimum wage (currently $719.35 per week before tax) and is paid by either your employer or the government (where employers do not provide parental leave entitlements).You can claim for paid parental leave up to three months in advance.

To be eligible you must have worked at least 330 hours across 10 of the 13 months prior to the birth of your child, but your annual salary must also be less than $150 000.The work test has been extended so that mothers can count periods of paid parental leave they've taken for earlier births as 'work'.

👍 TAX FACT

Paid parental leave is subject to income tax and may also affect other government benefits such as child support, health care cards and public housing. In contrast, the Newborn Upfront Payment and Supplement is not taxable and not considered income for family assistance or social security purposes. For more information on paid parental leave go to www. humanservices.gov.au/individuals/services/centrelink/parental-leave-pay.

👍 TAX FACT

Since 1 July 2016, parents are prevented from 'double-dipping' into parental leave, where they have simultaneous access to employer-funded benefits at the same level or more than the government scheme. If the employer-paid leave is less, then they will only receive the difference.

👍 TAX FACT

For children born after 1 March 2014, Family Tax Benefit Part A recipients may be entitled to a $550 Newborn Upfront Payment and up to $1649.83 for a Newborn Supplement (reduced to $1100.55 in total for subsequent children), payable via normal fortnightly payments over a three-month period. These payments are not taxable.

Dad and partner pay

To help partners bond with their new baby, eligible working partners of children born or adopted after 1 January 2013 may be entitled to a single 'dad and partner pay'. It is a one-off payment of up to two weeks at the national minimum wage (currently $719.35 per week before tax).

According to the Department of Human Services, you may be eligible to claim the Child Care Subsidy if you:

- had a child 13 or under and not attending secondary school
- passed the work/training/study test
- ensure that your children under seven either meet the Government's immunisation requirements or have an exemption
- used approved child care such as long day care, family day care, in-home care, outside school hours care, vacation care and/or some occasional care services.

Parents can claim up to 100 hours of CCS per child per fortnight dependent on passing a work/training/study test. Once eligible, the rebate is paid weekly or fortnightly by the Department of Human Services based on child care attendance information it receives electronically from your service provider. Even if your child is absent from child care, the Child Care Subsidy can still be paid in some situations. You can receive payments for up to 42 absences per financial year, if you are charged for child care. These absent days can be taken for any reason with no evidence required.

⚠ PITFALL

It is important to conservatively estimate your family income for the purposes of the Child Care Subsidy, because if you overestimate it you may need to pay back some or all of what you received during the year (even allowing for the 5% amounts previously withheld by the Department of Human Services).

🖕 TAX FACT

Since 1 July 2018 the Child Care Benefit and Child Care Rebate was abolished and replaced with the Child Care Subsidy (CCS).

7 LOW-INCOME EARNERS

There are a few tax benefits available if you are a low-income earner, such as when you work part time.

Low-income tax offset

The low-income tax offset (LITO) is a tax rebate for individuals on lower incomes. In 2019-20, the LITO will provide a tax rebate of $445 for individuals who earn less than $37 000. The offset is reduced by 1.5 cents for every dollar that your taxable income exceeds $37 000, before eroding entirely at $66 667.

To be eligible for LITO, you must be a resident for tax purposes and lodge a tax return. The ATO will automatically apply this offset to your assessment for you if you're entitled to it. Minors cannot use the LITO to reduce tax payable on their unearned income.

Low and middle income tax offset

In addition to LITO, the government introduced a new non-refundable low and middle income tax offset (LMITO) from 1 July 2018 to the 2021-22 year. The LMITO was proposed in the 2019-20 federal budget to provide an additional tax rebate of $255 for individuals who earn less than $37 000. The offset is increased by 7.5 cents for every dollar to $48 000 and stays at $1080 for taxable incomes up to $90 000. The offset is reduced by 1.5 cents for every dollar that your taxable income exceeds $90 000, before phasing out entirely at $126 000.

Superannuation co-contribution

If your total superannuation balance is under $1.6 million and your total income is under the low-income threshold of $38 564 and you contribute $1000 post-tax to your super fund, the government will match it by 50 per cent with a further $500. The super co-contribution gradually phases out to nil (by 3.333 cents per dollar) at the higher income threshold of $53 564.

Superannuation spouse contribution tax offset

You are entitled to a rebate of up to $540 if you make contributions into your spouse's superannuation fund, if your spouse's assessable income and reportable fringe benefits are less than $40 000.

The rebate is 18 per cent of the lesser of:

- $3000 reduced by $1 for every dollar that your spouse's assessable income and reportable fringe benefits exceed $37 000
- the total of the eligible spouse contribution.

Low-income superannuation tax offset

Since 1 July 2017 this offset replaced the Low-Income Superannuation Contribution but despite the new name, the operation remains the same. The government will contribute up to $500 annually into the superannuation account of workers on adjusted taxable incomes of up to $37 000 to ensure that no tax is paid on superannuation guarantee contributions.

8 SENIOR AND PENSIONER TAX OFFSET

Senior Australians or pensioners may be eligible for an offset that allows them to earn more income before they have to pay tax and the Medicare levy.

As we saw earlier, if you are under the pension age (currently 65.5 and increasing to 67 in 2023 and 70 by 2035), you can earn an income of up to $21 884 before any tax is payable (see p. 15).

The tax rules get even better when you reach age pension age (or service pension age), as you may be able to access more generous tax-free thresholds, known as the senior and pensioner tax offset (SAPTO). Table 1.5 shows the thresholds for the SAPTO.

TABLE 1.5: thresholds for senior and pensioner tax offsets (SAPTO) (2019–20)

	Maximum offset	Shaded-out threshold (taxable income)*	Cut-out threshold (taxable income)
Single	$2 230	$32 279	$50 119
Couple (each)	$1 602	$28 974**	$41 790**
Couple (combined)	$3 204	$57 948	$83 580
Couple (separated by illness)	$4 080	$62 558	$95 198

* Maximum offset reduced by 12.5 cents for each $1 in excess of shaded-out threshold.
** A taxpayer's taxable income is taken to be half the couple's combined taxable income.
Source: © Australian Taxation Office for the Commonwealth of Australia.

Senior Australians are not required to pay any income tax if their income is below $32 279 for singles (or $28 974 each for couples). But if senior Australians derive income from a share portfolio they are encouraged to lodge a tax return, as they will receive a nice refund from all of the excess franking credits attached to their dividends.

If you're single, you can earn up to $32 279 (and $28 974 each for couples) in non-super income without paying a cent of tax because of the application of SAPTO and LITO. Any additional superannuation benefit that you receive from a taxed source is tax-free.

Senior Australians who are over Age Pension age but still participate in the workforce can keep more of their pension when they have earnings from working via the Work Bonus incentive. The Work Bonus allows an eligible pensioner to earn an extra $250 per fortnight from employment (increasing to $300 from 1 July 2019) before it affects their pension rate. Single pensioners can effectively earn $422 per fortnight (being $250 from Work Bonus and the $172 income test free threshold) and still receive the maximum rate of pension.

Any unused part of the $250 fortnightly Work Bonus exemption amount can be accrued in a Work Bonus income bank, up to a maximum of $6500 (increasing to $7800 in 2019–20). The income bank amount is not time limited; if unused, it can carry forward into future years.

Senior Australians who are not eligible for a pension due to their income or assets, may still be eligible for a Commonwealth Seniors Health Card provided that they continue to reside in Australia and their adjusted taxable income is below:

- $54 929 a year if you're single
- $87 884 a year for couples
- $109 858 a year for couples separated by illness, respite care or prison

9 OTHER GOVERNMENT BENEFITS

There are so many different types of government benefits these days that it is no wonder some families are confused, and aren't claiming everything that they should be entitled to. Most entitlements are means tested, which means the benefits you receive are reduced as your income increases.

> **⚡ TIP**
>
> If you're in doubt when estimating your annual income, it is always better to overestimate. It can be difficult to repay a debt to Centrelink if you have already spent the cash!

Family Tax Benefit Part A

This benefit helps with the cost of raising dependent children and dependent full-time students under the age of 18. The amount of the benefit is determined by your family income as well as the number and age of your dependants. It will only be paid up to the end of the calendar year that your teenager is completing school.

Family Tax Benefit Part B

Restricted to families where the primary earner has an adjusted taxable income under $100 000, this benefit provides extra assistance to families with one main income. The lower-earning parent can earn up to $5621 per annum before the benefit reduces. The Family Tax Benefit Part B fades out when the secondary earner receives more than $27 722 income per annum.

Parenting payment

This payment provides financial help for people who are the primary carers of children. It is means tested on both your income and assets.

Better start for children with a disability

Families with children under the age of six who have been diagnosed with sight or hearing impairments, cerebral palsy, Down syndrome, fragile X syndrome, Prader Willi syndrome, Williams syndrome, Angelman syndrome, Kabuki syndrome, Smith-Magenis syndrome, CHARGE syndrome, Cornelia de Lange syndrome, Rett's Disorder, Cri du Chat syndrome or microcephaly are eligible for funding towards early intervention.

The $12 000 early intervention funding (capped at $6000 per annum) is paid to service providers on a fee-for-services basis via the Department of Social Services (DSS). Families living in outer regional or remote areas may be eligible for an additional one-off payment of $2000.

Youth Allowance

The Youth Allowance is a government benefit paid to eligible students, apprentices or those looking for work aged 16 to 24. It is means tested based on both the young person's income and his or her parents' income. The allowance is assessable and must be included in your income tax return. Unfortunately, Youth Allowance recipients cannot claim a tax deduction for expenses incurred in relation to their studies.

Transition to work

Transition to Work provides pre-employment help to eligible young job seekers who are aged between 15 and 21 years, and are not involved in study or work. Eligibility is only available if the young job seeker does not have a Year 12 (or equivalent) or Certificate III qualification.

Pension loans scheme

If you or your partner are of Age Pension age, you own real estate in Australia and you receive less than the maximum rate of the Age (or Disability Support or Widow B) Pension, then you can apply for a non-taxable loan if you need extra income or to help for a short time or an indefinite period. The loan is capped up to the maximum rate of pension, paid fortnightly.

> **⚠ PITFALL**
>
> Although the 2018–19 federal budget has proposed extending the eligibility of the Pension Loans Scheme to everyone over Age Pension age that has real estate, as an additional maximum fortnightly income stream up to 150 per cent of the Age Pension rate, the loan is accruing interest at a rate (currently 5.25 per cent) higher than what banks lend at. Whilst we all know of the benefits of compound interest when saving, with no minimum repayment back to the government, there can be sizable detriment as interest is charged on interest over time.

> **⚠ PITFALL**
>
> Under the gifting rules, the maximum amount that you can gift to a friend or relative is $10 000 in each financial year and $30 000 in total over the previous five-year period. Any excess amounts are added back as part of your assets under the assets test.

Other benefits

The following additional benefits may also be available to families:

- energy supplement
- single income family supplement
- telephone allowance
- multiple birth allowance
- rent assistance
- health care card.

10 FAMILY BREAKDOWN

While we all want to have the perfect marriage and live happily ever after, the sad reality is that approximately one-third of marriages end in divorce in Australia.

The tax system has provisions in place to assist with easing the financial burden of separating families. These provisions apply to capital gains tax (CGT), superannuation and income from child- and partner-support payments.

Transfer of assets

Normally, when you sell an asset that was acquired after 19 September 1985, you are liable for CGT. However, when you transfer assets to your spouse as a result of the breakdown of your relationship, it is classified as an 'automatic rollover' of those assets and you will not have to pay CGT at that time. Any subsequent disposal of the asset will trigger the CGT provisions, except for the family home, which is exempt.

> **👆 TAX FACT**
>
> There is no CGT if you transfer a property to your former spouse under a court order following the breakdown of your marriage.

This rollover ensures the spouse who gives the assets disregards a capital gain or capital loss that would otherwise arise, and the one who receives the asset (the transferee spouse) will make the capital gain or capital loss when they subsequently dispose of the asset.

> **⚠ PITFALL**
>
> If you and your spouse divide your property under a private or informal agreement (not because of a court order, a binding financial agreement, an arbitral award or another agreement or award), marriage or relationship breakdown rollover does not apply.

Transfer of superannuation

The splitting of superannuation between divorcing partners is similarly treated as a rollover. As the funds are not being released as a payment, this rollover split does not need to wait until retirement.

Child support and spouse support payments

You do not need to include any child support or spouse support payments that you may receive in your taxable income, but they are part of your adjusted taxable income calculation for tax offset purposes. Similarly, there is no tax deduction available for child support or spouse support payments.

The ATO cooperates with the Child Support Agency to:

- supply information to the Child Support Agency for the purpose of calculating child support payments
- encourage lodgement of outstanding tax returns
- recoup child-support debt from tax returns.

Some may say that binding financial agreements defeat the purpose of marrying based on the values of love and trust, but seeking legal advice on setting up a binding financial agreement could be a good preventative measure against a bag egg. Love hurts, but divorce can be expensive. Make sure you consult a lawyer before drafting up any such agreement.

There are many benefits to using trusts to manage your wealth, including:

- *Asset protection.* Family assets may be protected from 'creditors and predators' in the event of bankruptcy or insolvency in certain situations.
- *Australia-wide.* A trust established under Australian law can operate effectively in every Australian state. If you have potential beneficiaries living overseas, it is recommended that you seek specialist advice before proceeding further as there are many tax implications to consider.
- *Flexibility.* Trust deeds are flexible in their operation and can cater for a wide variety of beneficiary classes and investments, and different types of income can be directed to different beneficiaries.
- *Little regulation.* Trusts do not have as many reporting requirements and obligations as company structures.
- *Tax minimisation.* Income can be directed to family members on lower tax rates.

If you place money in a term deposit, consider having it mature after 30 June so that any income is not assessable until the following financial year.

PART II

YOUR EMPLOYMENT

There have been a few noticeable changes in employment conditions in recent years. Employees seem to be working longer hours as employers seek greater productivity. Employees also seem to be bearing the greater brunt of expenses as employers have become more cost-driven and hence a lot less generous in reimbursing work-related expenses.

👍 TAX FACT

Of the 13.87 million people who lodged a tax return in 2016–17, just over 8.8 million claimed $21.986 billion in deductions for work-related expenses.

Fortunately, employees can claim for work-related expenses in their income tax return each year and get a refund at their marginal rate of tax.

👍 TAX FACT

If you work in one of the following occupations or industries, make sure you look at the relevant ATO publication on claiming specific work-related expenses in your tax return:

- adult industry workers
- airline employees
- Australian Defence Force members
- building and construction workers and earthmoving plant operators
- cleaners
- doctor, specialist or other medical professionals
- education professionals
- electricians
- engineers

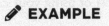 **EXAMPLE**

Danielle works for a department store in the city and is required to attend a meeting at her employer's other store in the suburbs and travels in her own car. As the meeting finishes late she travels directly home from the meeting. She can claim the cost of the journey from the city store to the suburban store and from the alternative workplace to her home.

The following three characteristics will assist you in determining if your work is itinerant:

- travel is a fundamental part of your work
- you have a web of workplaces in your regular employment with no fixed place of work
- you regularly work at more than one site each day before returning home.

EXAMPLE

David is employed as a plumber's labourer and works at different sites each day. He travels directly from home to a different site each day to start work. The travel between sites on a regular basis is an integral part of his job and thus his employment would be considered by the ATO to be itinerant.

However, a builder's labourer who works at a single building site for a few months before moving on to another site is not engaged in itinerant work.

⚠ PITFALL

Common mistakes made with car claims include:
- a lack of evidence to support claims
- providing a 'rough estimate' of your business usage
- deductions being incorrectly claimed for the costs of travel between home and work.

I am a painter by trade and recently purchased a brand new ute. I work full time and carry my gear with me at all times. I want to know what I can claim, and if I have to keep a log book even though I use my vehicle 100 per cent for work.

Given that you have a ute (commercial vehicle greater than 1 tonne) and clearly carry paint gear all the time, there is no requirement to maintain a logbook as it would be considered 100 per cent work use. However, if you want to use the logbook method then you will need to keep all receipts throughout the year for expenses such as petrol, registration, insurance, servicing and repairs as well as any finance payments (lease or interest).

14 METHODS TO CLAIM CAR TRAVEL

There are only two specific methods available to individuals to calculate deductions for car expenses:

- cents per kilometre method
- logbook (12-week) method

♀ TIP

If you often use your car for work, the logbook method is probably your best option for calculating deductions.

If you use the logbook method, purchase a logbook from the newsagent, fill it out for a continuous 12-week period and keep records of all costs associated with the running of your car including petrol, registration, insurances, servicing, repairs, lease payments, batteries, tyres, and so on. The hard work is worth it as deductions can be in the thousands and you only need to do a new logbook every five years unless you change your job or car.

Under the logbook method, you can claim a portion of the running costs of the car, including depreciation and interest, based upon your work-related use percentage.

⚠ PITFALL

The ATO does check logbooks for their authenticity and a common error is a lack of evidence to support a claim. Each work-related business trip must be entered at the end of the journey (or as soon as possible afterwards) and show:

- the date
- kilometres travelled
- opening and closing odometer readings
- the purpose of the journey.

Under the cents per kilometre method, you must make a reasonable estimate of kilometres travelled, up to a maximum of 5000, and multiply this by a flat rate of 68 cents per kilometre, regardless of engine capacity.

You need to satisfy the tax office that the travel was undertaken for income-producing purposes and that your claim is calculated on a reasonable basis. Do not guess!

✏ EXAMPLE

George is a mechanic who is required to travel regularly to pick up spare parts from a supplier. In his tax return, he guesses that he travelled 3500 kilometres.

A check with George's employer reveals that the trip to the supplier is an 8-kilometre round-trip journey, made no more than three days per week and that George also had four weeks' holidays during the year.

George has not made a reasonable estimate and the claim should have been based on 1152 kilometres (three days × 8 km × 48 weeks). Based on a two-litre engine, the deduction that can be claimed is $783 (1152 km × 68 cents).

> **👆 TAX FACT**
>
> Under the logbook method, you can claim fuel and oil costs on either your actual receipts or an estimate based on odometer readings from the start and the end of the year.

> **⚠ PITFALL**
>
> If you purchase a car for more than $57 581, the ATO will limit your deduction for depreciation to the first $57 581. While I say all cars cost money, they cost even more if they are expensive luxury cars (as you don't even get a tax break on the excess that you are paying).

15 TRAVEL

If you incur travel expenses in the course of your work, or in travelling between one place of business and another, they are deductible — for example motor vehicle expenses, air, bus, train or taxi fares, and car rental costs. Accommodation and meals on business trips away from home may also be deductible.

> **⚠ PITFALL**
>
> Passport fees and travel insurance are generally considered to be private in nature and are not deductible.

> **💡 TIP**
>
> If you want to claim travel expenses, you need to keep a travel diary. This applies to work-related trips interstate or overseas of more than five days. It must detail dates, places, times and duration of activities and travel. It's also a good idea to keep business cards of contacts you meet and, even better, give a presentation or a report on your trip when you get back to work that includes this information.

There are special substantiation requirements to making a successful travel tax claim.

A travel diary is a separate record of activities undertaken during travel. Its purpose is to show which of the activities were for income-producing purposes so that an appropriate classification can be made between deductible and non-deductible expenses. An activity is recorded by specifying its:

- date and approximate start time
- duration
- location
- nature.

Note that the requirement to keep travel records in the form of a diary is separate from the requirement to obtain written evidence of travel expenses.

👍 TAX FACT

Sometimes taxpayers mix business with pleasure and it is not uncommon to tack on a personal holiday at the end of an overseas conference. However, travel expenses related to attending conferences, seminars and other work-related events are deductible only to the extent that they relate to your income-producing activities.

You will need to apportion your travel expenses where you undertake both work-related and private activities. Travel costs to and from an overseas conference will only be deductible where the main purpose of the travel was to attend the event. Accommodation, food and other incidental costs must be apportioned between work-related and private activities taking into account your activities on the day you incurred the cost.

Some employers pay a travel allowance to cover expenses for accommodation, food, drink or incidentals incurred by an employee while travelling away from home overnight. If your employer does this and the allowance is less than the reasonable travel allowance published by the ATO, you can claim a deduction for the amount of the allowance without further substantiation.

16 UNIFORM

The cost of certain types of work clothing may be deductible, as may the cost of buying or replacing clothing, uniforms and footwear. But a deduction is only available if the clothing is one of the following:

- protective
- a compulsory uniform to be worn for work
- a non–compulsory uniform that has been entered on the Register of Approved Occupational Clothing.

Tax deductions for the costs of washing, drying or ironing clothes are only available for clothing that falls into one or more of the above categories.

The ATO considers the following to meet the definition of protective clothing:

- fire-resistant and sun-protection clothing
- safety-coloured vests
- non-slip nurse's shoes
- rubber boots for concreters
- steel-capped boots, gloves, overalls, and heavy-duty shirts and trousers
- overalls, smocks and aprons you wear to avoid damage or soiling to your ordinary clothes during your income-earning activities.

If you do your own laundry you can claim $1 per load if the load is made up only of eligible clothes (and includes the washing, drying and ironing of them). This reduces to 50 cents per load if other laundry items are included. If your total laundry costs exceed $150 you must be able to substantiate your claim.

All other expenditure on clothing and its maintenance is considered a private expenditure and is not deductible.

💡 TIP

A deduction for uniformed clothing is only available if it is protective clothing or compulsory, unique and distinctive. Non-compulsory uniforms must be entered on the Register of Approved Occupational Clothing in order to be deductible.

There must be a clear connection between the clothing expenditure and income-earning activities in order to obtain a deduction. In general you cannot claim a deduction for conventional clothing that forms part of a uniform even if your employer requires you to wear it.

✏️ EXAMPLE

A businessman wearing a business suit and tie or a sales assistant working for a big fashion label and wearing one of their tops as a condition of employment are not wearing clothes that are deductible.

Clothing purchased by a taxpayer is considered conventional if it is not distinctive or unique, can be worn on any occasion—including private and social occasions—and is easily available to the public.

17 HOME OFFICE

More and more people these days are doing work at home as an easy remedy to balance the conflicting pressures of work and family. If you perform some of your work from your home office, you may be able to claim a deduction for the costs you incur in running your home office, even if the room is not set aside solely for work-related purposes.

You may be able to claim the work-related portion of:

- depreciation of home-office furniture, fittings and equipment such as computers and desks—if your equipment costs less than $300, you can claim a full deduction for the work-related portion
- home telephone calls
- home telephone rental if:
  - you are on call
  - you have to phone your employer, clients or students regularly while you are away from your workplace

- internet access charges
- printer and printer cartridges
- stationery
- the cost of heating, cooling and lighting your home office that is over the amount you would ordinarily have to pay if you did not work from home
- the costs of repairs to your home-office furniture and fittings.

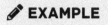

Sit at your desk at home and scan the room for the various items that you may use, even partially, for work purposes.

✎ EXAMPLE

Shelby uses her computer and personal internet account at home to access her work emails and to grade student assignments in the following percentages:

- 35 per cent for work purposes
- 65 per cent for private purposes.

This means Shelby can claim 35 per cent of both the depreciation of her computer and her internet costs.

⚠ PITFALL

If your income is paid to you as an employee, you are generally not able to claim a deduction for your occupancy expenses including:

- council rates
- home insurance premiums
- mortgage interest
- rent.

You can only claim occupancy expenses where your home office is considered to be a place of business.

According to the ATO, to claim a deduction for electricity and gas and the decline in value of home-office furniture you can use either of the following:

- your actual expenses
- a rate of 52 cents per hour.

✎ EXAMPLE

Michelle uses a diary to record the time she uses her home office for work purposes. Based on her diary entries, Michelle works out that she spends an average of four hours each weeknight working in her home office. Michelle works for 46 weeks each year.

Michelle calculates her home-office running expense deduction as follows:

46 weeks × 20 hours × 0.52 cents = $478

🎁 BONUS RESOURCES

Go to my website www.mrtaxman.com.au for a home-office expenses calculator to help you work out how much you can claim.

18 OTHER WORK-RELATED DEDUCTIONS

Other work-related expenses that you incur as an employee that haven't been mentioned previously may include:

- briefcases
- calculators and personal organisers
- diaries and logbooks
- first-aid courses
- income-protection insurances
- interest on money borrowed to finance work-related purchases
- mobile phones
- overtime meal expenses
- postage
- professional seminars, courses, conferences and workshops
- reference books
- stationery
- subscriptions
- sun protection
- technical journals, periodicals and magazines
- tools of trade
- union fees.

♀ TIP

It is better to get your employer to pay for as many work-related expenses as possible rather than claiming them yourself. Based on the marginal tax rates, you only get back a percentage of any expense incurred, not 100 per cent of the expense. Avoid leaving yourself out of pocket.

The records you must keep to substantiate your claims include:

- receipts or other written evidence of your expenses, including receipts for depreciating assets you have purchased
- diary entries you make to record your small expenses ($10 or less) totalling no more than $200, or expenses that you cannot obtain any kind of evidence for, regardless of the amount — for example, stationery
- itemised phone accounts that detail work-related calls — if you don't receive itemised accounts, you can make a reasonable estimate of your call costs based on diary records you have kept over a four-week period, together with your relevant telephone accounts.

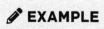 EXAMPLE

Lucy uses her mobile phone for work purposes. She is on a mobile phone plan of $49 per month and rarely exceeds the plan cap. She reviews an itemised account for one month from her phone provider, which includes details of the individual calls she has made. She highlights the work-related calls she has made and makes notes on her account about who she is calling for work and personal purposes — her employer, parents, and so on.

She works out that 45 per cent of the individual call expenses are for work and applies that to her cap amount of $49 a month. Reviews of other months are consistent with this.

If Lucy only worked for 26 weeks of the year, she would calculate her work-related mobile phone expense deduction as follows:

$$6 \text{ months} \times \$49 \times 0.45 = \$132$$

⚠ PITFALL

If you have purchased any assets that cost more than $300 you must depreciate them rather than claim the full amount as an immediate deduction.

Can you claim for expenses incurred that have been purchased via the National Disability Insurance Scheme?

Unfortunately you cannot claim deductions for expenses incurred (or for assets purchased) in relation to any exempt income, including amounts received from the NDIS.

19 KEEPING THOSE RECEIPTS

It is crucial that you keep your receipts, particularly as the ATO increases its audit activity all the time. With the ATO motto of 'no receipt means no deduction' you could be missing out on legitimate tax deductions by not keeping good records.

Under the Australian tax system of self-assessment you are responsible for working out how much you can claim on your tax return. In order to prepare an accurate tax return and support the claims you make, you need to keep careful records.

Personally I don't care what system you use to keep your receipts ... just have one, although I will say that the ATO have developed an excellent *myDeductions* app that you could use. The system that works will be organised into various categories to allow you to find a receipt within five minutes if asked.

♀ TIP

If you are struggling to keep a record of your tax deductions during the year, simply download the ATO's *myDeductions* app to your smart device and make it easier and more convenient at tax time. You can add:

- deductions/expenses
- vehicle trips
- income (if you're a sole trader)
- photos of your invoices and receipts.

Most accountants prefer that you don't give them a shoebox each year, but instead a typed-up summary, perhaps in Excel, of your income and expenses. Their tax agent fees may even fall as a result!

If you're not sure whether or not to keep a record, you should keep it—it is better to have too many than not enough.

⚲ TIP

It doesn't matter what system you use to keep your tax receipts, just make sure you use one! An Excel spreadsheet showing your income and expenses works for many people.

If your total claims add up to more than $300, you must keep written evidence, such as receipts, bank statements and credit card statements. You must be able to show evidence you have incurred the full amount of your claim, not just the amount over the first $300.

Written evidence should show:

- amount of the expense
- date you incurred the expense
- nature of the goods or services—if this is not shown, you can write this on the document before you lodge your income tax return
- supplier's name.

If the total amount you are claiming is $300 or less, you do not need to keep receipts.

⚠ PITFALL

Even if you hold onto the original receipt, there is no tax deduction available if you have been reimbursed by your employer.

YOUR EMPLOYMENT 45

Generally, you must keep your written evidence for five years from:

- the date the notice of assessment is sent to you
- the date of your last claim for any decline in value for depreciating assets
- disposal of an asset for CGT purposes
- the date a dispute with the ATO is finalised.

👆 TAX FACT

Taxpayers with 'simple tax affairs' only need to retain their records for two years if:

- their income consists only of salary or wages, interest or dividends within Australia
- deductions are only for managing tax affairs, bank fees or donations.

Documents that you are required to keep can be in written or electronic form. If you make copies they must be a true and clear reproduction of the original.

⚠ PITFALL

If you keep records electronically, be very careful about not losing that data. A regular back-up is essential to ensure that the evidence is easily accessible if a hard drive is corrupted or a computer stolen.

20 ATO HIT LISTS

Every year, based on an analysis of previous returns, the ATO issues a 'hit list' of occupations that will be targeted for close attention regarding work-related expenses.

👆 TAX FACT

The ATO's tactic of putting the spotlight on particular groups has proven successful in past years. When the ATO targets particular industries, its tax collection improves by 22 per cent.

Generally the ATO looks closely at a range of claims for deductions including expenses for motor vehicles, self-education and travel. It also looks at tax returns from previous years and identifies particular occupations to put under the microscope where:

- average amounts of claims are high
- there is an increase in the number of people making claims
- there are a lot of people making claims for the first time.

In the spirit of 'prevention is much better than cure', the ATO uses that information and writes to people in those occupations. It sends information outlining common mistakes made in claims, and provides help on how people can get their claims right in the subsequent year's tax return.

⚠ PITFALL

The ATO is aware of scam emails that appear to be from an @ato.gov.au email address and display as being sent from the 'Australian Tax Office'. If you have received emails from this source do not open the attachment and delete the email immediately. If the ATO needs to contact you they will only do so via the phone or post.

♀ TIP

While the natural tendency of people in targeted occupations is to reduce the amount of their claims out of fear, if you are genuinely entitled to a legitimate tax deduction then you should claim it. By all means go to the boundary, but not over it. If you are concerned about your claims then you should seek advice from a tax expert.

The first step in a subsequent ATO investigation usually involves a 'please explain' letter requesting further information about your tax return.

Usually a person is given 28 days to respond and the ATO might also ask for copies of receipts and other supporting documents. Only if the matter remains unresolved after this is a face-to-face meeting required.

You will be given lots of opportunity to explain yourself. But the penalties are significant so it's best to have all your affairs in order. Penalties start from a minor adjustment to your return if there was a genuine mistake or misinterpretation of the law, and escalate to severe fines.

⚠ PITFALL

If you make a downright fraudulent claim for, say, $20 000 and there is no substance at all to it, the ATO can charge up to 90 per cent tax in penalties, plus an interest penalty on top of that.

👍 TAX FACT

The ATO has outlined some simple rules for getting your work-related expenses claim correct:

- You must have incurred the expense in the year you are claiming for.
- The expense must be work-related and not private.
- Receiving an allowance from your employer does not automatically entitle you to a deduction.
- If your claims total more than $300 you need written evidence.

Penalties that the ATO can charge as a percentage of any tax shortfall are 75 per cent for intentional disregard of a tax law; 50 per cent for recklessness; and 25 per cent when you don't take reasonable care, if your case is not reasonably argued or if you disregard a private ruling by the ATO. These penalties are increased by a further 20 per cent of the base amount if you do not cooperate and make it difficult for the ATO when looking at your affairs (for example, the penalty for intentional disregard of a tax law when you don't cooperate becomes 90 per cent, being 120 per cent of the base penalty of 75 per cent). The Commissioner encourages voluntary disclosure so if you confess your sins during an audit investigation they will reduce the base penalty amount by 20 per cent. If you advise of any errors prior to any audit activity, then the base penalty amount is reduced by 80 per cent.

21 REDUNDANCY

Over the past five years there has been plenty of uncertainty in the global economy with many people still experiencing job losses as the fallout from the global financial crisis (GFC) continues.

If there can be any good news it relates to your favourable tax treatment if you have been dismissed from your employment and received a genuine redundancy payment.

Tax-free component of genuine redundancy

Part of a genuine redundancy is tax-free and must be taken in cash. The tax-free limit for the 2019–20 income year is $10 638 plus a further $5320 for each completed year of service.

Balance of redundancy

Anything in excess of the tax-free amount is treated as an 'employment termination payment'. The first $210 000 in 2019–20 is taxed at 17 per cent if you are over 57, or 32 per cent if you are under 57. Any excess payment is taxed at 47 per cent. These tax breaks will only apply to the part of a payment that, when combined with other taxable income, does not exceed $180 000.

> ♀ **TIP**
>
> The balance of a genuine redundancy can be rolled over into your superannuation fund as a personal contribution and is then concessionally taxed at only 15 per cent within the fund.

Unused leave entitlements

Only 5 per cent of any unused annual or long-service leave that relates to service prior to 16 August 1978 is taxed at your marginal rate. If you leave employment because of a genuine redundancy, invalidity or early retirement scheme, then the balance is taxed at 32 per cent. You cannot roll any unused leave entitlements over into your super fund. Note that the tax calculation on unused leave entitlements is different if you leave employment for any other reason.

> ✎ **EXAMPLE**
>
> Natalie, aged 51, is made redundant on 30 June 2018 after working at her company since 15 February 2008. Her company pays her $130 000 as a genuine redundancy plus her unused leave entitlements, which come to another $31 234.
>
> As she has given the company 10 full years of service, the tax-free component of her genuine redundancy is $63 838 ($10 638 + [$5320 ×10]) and the balance of $66 162 is an employment termination payment.
>
> As she is only 51, and doesn't elect to roll over any money into her super fund, the $66 162 is taxed at 32 per cent; that is, $21 172. Her unused leave entitlements are taxed at 32 per cent; that is, $9995.

22 WORKING A SECOND JOB

Tax problems always seem to occur when you start working a second job. If you are an Australian resident for tax purposes, the first $18 200 of your yearly income is not taxed. This is called the tax-free threshold. You can claim the tax-free threshold from one payer only when you complete your *TFN declaration* (NAT 3092).

You should claim the tax-free threshold with the payer who pays the highest wage. If you earn any additional income from a second job your other payer is required to withhold tax at a higher rate.

If you are currently claiming the tax-free threshold with a payer and you want to claim it from a new payer, you must advise your first payer that you no longer wish to claim the tax-free threshold by completing a withholding declaration (NAT 3093).

Where an insufficient amount of tax is being withheld, you can directly instruct a payer to withhold a higher amount of tax, by supplying them with a completed *Withholding declaration — upwards variation* (NAT 5367) form. However, if your payer is withholding tax at the prescribed rates, you are under no obligation to increase the amount of tax being withheld. You suffer no penalty at the end of the financial year, other than having to find a further amount of money to pay your tax.

✐ EXAMPLE

Stuart is employed in two part-time jobs. He receives $30 000 from the first job and claims the tax-threshold and $18 000 from the second job but does not claim any threshold. Using the ATO's *Pay- as-you-go (PAYG) withholding — Fortnightly tax table* (NAT 1006), the tax withheld on Stuart's wages is outlined in table 2.1.

TABLE 2.1: example — tax withheld

	Annual income	Fortnightly income	Tax withheld
First job	$30 000	$1153.85	$108
Second job	$18 000	$692.31	$156
Total	$48 000	$1846.16	$264

Source: © Australian Taxation Office for the Commonwealth of Australia.

At the end of the financial year Stuart's net tax position is:

Income tax on $48 000	$7147
Medicare levy (2%)	$960
Total tax payable	**$8107**
Less: LITO & LMITO	$535
Less: tax withheld ($264 × 26)	$6864
Net tax shortfall	**$708**

To avoid this situation, Stuart can either put money aside for when his income tax assessment is issued or choose to ask one or both of his employers to withhold extra tax to cover the shortfall.

If you think you are having too much tax withheld from one of your wages, you can arrange for a PAYG withholding variation form to be completed and reduce the amount withheld from your regular pay. Or wait until the end of the year and get a nice refund.

♀ TIP

When you have a second job you may be able to claim the cost of travelling directly between two separate places of employment. However, you can't claim the cost of travelling from your second job to your home.

23 SALARY SACRIFICE

It is quite common for employees to set up a salary-sacrifice arrangement with their employer and 'package' some of their future salary or wages in return for benefits of a similar value provided by their employer. These benefits may include superannuation and fringe benefits such as company cars, private health insurance and other expense payments.

👆 TAX FACT

Your income tax liability should be less under a salary-sacrifice arrangement than it would have been without entering into the agreement. It is important to note, though, that there are some associated costs that you need to consider before entering into any arrangement. These costs may include the opportunity cost of the amount being sacrificed plus any surcharges which may arise after having the benefits reported on your payment summary.

Provided that any benefits form part of your remuneration, there is no limit on the amount or the types of benefits that can be sacrificed. They are simply replacing what otherwise could have been paid as salary.

💡 TIP

Superannuation, exempt fringe benefits and some car fringe benefits are generally the best forms of salary sacrifice for tax purposes.

Salary-sacrificed superannuation contributions under an effective salary-sacrifice arrangement are considered to be employer contributions and are taxed at 15 per cent (increasing to 30 per cent for individuals with income greater than $250 000, subject to contribution limits, within the fund. This is a lot more tax-effective than paying 47 per cent tax on your cash salary, if you are on the highest marginal tax rate.

The following — limited to one per year — are exempt benefits:

- briefcase
- computer software
- portable electronic device (unlimited for small businesses)
- protective clothing
- tools of the trade.

There are two alternative methods to calculate the FBT for cars:

- Logbook — based on actual usage over a 12-week period completed in the past five years.
- Statutory method — based on the total number of kilometres travelled and applying a statutory fraction to the cost of the car provided. Table 2.2 shows the fractions that apply and have been replaced with a flat rate of 20 per cent for all cars acquired after 1 April 2014.

TABLE 2.2: car fringe benefits statutory formula rates (2019–20)

| | Statutory fraction of car base value | | | | |
| | Date contract entered into | | | | |
Travel (kms)	Before 11/5/11	11/5/11 – 31/3/12	1/4/12 – 31/3/13	1/4/13 – 31/3/14	After 1/4/14
0–14 999	26%	20%	20%	20%	20%
15 000–24 999	20%	20%	20%	20%	20%
25 000–40 000	11%	14%	17%	20%	20%
40 001 and over	7%	10%	13%	17%	20%

Source: © Australian Taxation Office for the Commonwealth of Australia.

Reportable fringe benefits amounts are certain fringe benefits greater than $2000 which are included in your payment summary and shown in your tax return, but not included in your assessable income. They are included in a number of income tests for certain government benefits including:

- Medicare levy surcharge
- deductions for personal super contributions
- super co-contributions
- spouse super contributions
- HELP and Financial Supplement repayments
- child-support obligations.

✎ EXAMPLE

Table 2.3 illustrates the way salary sacrificing and employee contributions work. Aaron earns $74000 a year. He has a car purchased for $40000 which has annual running expenses of $15000. If he travels 22000 kilometres during the FBT year, the taxable value of the car fringe benefit will be $8000 (20 per cent × $40000) and he will need to sacrifice one of the following:

- $22094 without any employee contributions
- $7000 if employee contributions of $8000 are made.

TABLE 2.3: example — salary sacrifice

	1 Salary only (no packaging)	2 Salary + car (without employee contributions)	3 Salary + car (with employee contributions)
Annual remuneration	$74000	$74000	$74000
Less salary sacrifice	Nil	$22094	$7000
Taxable income	**$74000**	**$51906**	**$67000**
Less income tax	$15597	$8416	$13322
Less Medicare levy	$1480	$1038	$1340
Add LMITO	$1080	$1080	$1080
Income after tax/ salary sacrifice	**$58003**	**$43532**	**$53418**
Less employee contribution	Nil	Nil	$8000
Less car expenses	$15000	Nil	Nil
Net disposable income	**$43003**	**$43532**	**$45418**
Reportable fringe benefits amount (taxable value × 1.8868)	Nil	$15094	Nil

Source: © Australian Taxation Office for the Commonwealth of Australia.

> **⚠ PITFALL**
>
> Since 1 April 2016, the government placed a grossed-up $5000 cap on the amount of salary-sacrificed 'meal entertainment' and 'entertainment facility leasing expenses' which qualify for an FBT exemption or rebate.

25 LIVING-AWAY-FROM-HOME ALLOWANCE

The ATO defines a living-away-from-home allowance (LAFHA) as a taxable allowance that an employer pays to an employee to compensate for additional expenses incurred and any disadvantages suffered because the employee is required to live away from their usual place of residence in order to perform their employment-related duties.

You are considered to be living away from your usual place of residence when:

- you change your job location (but not your employer)
- you intend to return to your original location after time away
- the period away exceeds 21 days.

As a practical general rule, where the period away does not exceed 21 days, the allowance will be treated as a travelling allowance rather than as a LAFHA.

FBT is only payable on the amount that the LAFHA exceeds the exempt accommodation and food components.

Since 1 January 2017, working holiday makers (that is, backpackers with either 417 or 462 visa subclass) are taxed at 15 per cent for the first $37 000 of their income. As table 2.4 shows, the subsequent 'backpacker tax' is at the same rates as residents on incomes above $37 000

TABLE 2.4: tax rates for working holiday makers excluding levies (2019–20)

Taxable income	Tax on this income
$0–$37 000	15c for each $1
$37 001–$90 000	$5550 plus 32.5c for each $1 over $37 000
$90 001–$180 000	$22 775 plus 37c for each $1 over $90 000
$180 001 and over	$56 075 plus 45c for each $1 over $180 000

Source: © Australian Taxation Office for the Commonwealth of Australia.

Since 1 October 2012, LAFHA can only be claimed by people who maintain a home for their own use in Australia that they are living away from for work. In addition, the LAFHA concession can only be used for the expenses of people who are legitimately maintaining a second home in addition to their actual home for a maximum period of 12 months. For those Australian residents who had an employment arrangement in place before 8 May 2012 (that has not been materially varied), then the new LAFHA rules have been applicable since 1 July 2014.

You have not made a material change to your employment arrangement if:

- your salary is adjusted as a result of an annual salary review (or other annual adjustments are made)
- you are promoted and the underlying terms of your employment arrangement do not change.

Accommodation

The exempt accommodation component of the LAFHA is the amount you pay for additional accommodation expenses you could reasonably be expected to incur at the alternative location. The ATO doesn't have any strict guidelines concerning what is considered 'reasonable accommodation', but it mainly boils down to common sense. Factors you could take into account when determining the accommodation cost include:

- whether you will be accompanied by family members
- the position you hold
- the location where you will be living
- whether the accommodation will be furnished
- your current living standards.

> **⚠ PITFALL**
>
> If an employee does not spend all of the LAFHA provided for accommodation, the excess is not an exempt accommodation component and is taxable for FBT purposes.

Food

The exempt food component is the amount of the LAFHA that is compensation for expenses you could reasonably be expected to incur on food and drink because you must live away from your usual place of residence, less the statutory food amount of $42 a week for each adult (12 years old and above) and $21 a week for each child (under 12 at the beginning of the year).

There are no strict guidelines as to how the food component is calculated, provided the amount is reasonable. You could determine reasonable food costs using the rates the ATO publishes each year for expatriates, providing they are reasonable in your circumstances. The acceptable amounts for the reasonable food component in the 2019–20 financial year of LAFHAs for expatriate employees, per ATO Tax Determination 2019/7, are as follows:

- one adult $269
- two adults $404
- three adults $539
- one adult + one child $337
- two adults + one child $472
- two adults + two children $540
- two adults + three children $608
- three adults + one child $607
- three adults + two children $675
- four adults $674
- additional adult $135
- additional child $68.

⚠ PITFALL

457 visa holders do not satisfy the requirement of maintaining a home for their own use in Australia while they are living away from it. As a result, they are not able to claim deductions for accommodation and food, but will still need to include any allowance received as assessable income. For those 457 visa holders who had an employment arrangement in place before 8 May 2012 (which has not been materially varied), then the new LAFHA rules have been applicable since 1 July 2014.

👆 TAX FACT

If you are an employee who works on a 'fly-in fly-out' or a 'drive-in drive-out' basis (such as a miner), then you are not subject to the same 'maximum 12 months' LAFHA rule. You will still need to substantiate your accommodation and food expenses if they are more than the ATO's reasonable amounts.

PART III

YOUR EDUCATION

Contrary to what many property experts and stockbrokers may tell you, the best investment that you could make is in yourself. With the economy recovering there are going to be some great opportunities in the job market for those who have acquired more skills. You are never too old to learn new tricks and, as my old man would say, nobody can take your education away from you.

👆 TAX FACT

Of the 539 000 taxpayers that claimed for self-education expenses in 2016–17, 68 per cent earned less than $80 000 for the year.

Australia is in the midst of an education revolution and pushing for more highly skilled workers. Tax and government incentives are helping fill the classrooms of universities and technical and further education (TAFE) colleges around the country with part-time students every evening. Employers are also expecting more from their employees and encouraging them to study in conjunction with their work.

💡 TIP

If you are planning to claim self-education expenses, be sure that the course you are claiming specifically relates to a current income-producing role, not one you hope to have in the future.

This part focuses on the financial implications and government incentives around studying.

26 CLAIMING SELF-EDUCATION EXPENSES

Work-related self-education expenses are the costs you incur to undertake a work-related course of study at a school, college, university or other recognised place of education.

👍 TAX FACT

The ATO says a tax deduction for your self-education expenses is available if you work and study at the same time, the course has sufficient connection to your current employment, and it *either*:

- maintains or improves the specific skills or knowledge you require in your current employment
  or
- results in, or is likely to result in, an increase in your income from your current employment.

According to the ATO, if a course of study is too general in terms of your current income-earning activities, the necessary connection between the self-education expense and your income-earning activity does not exist.

⚠ PITFALL

The ATO is quite strict in its view on self-education expense deductions. A deduction for self-education expenses cannot be claimed for a course that does not have a sufficient connection to your current employment even if the course:

- is generally related to your current employment
- enables you to get new employment.

Provided there is sufficient connection between your course and employment at the time you incurred the expense, the following self-education expenses are allowable tax deductions:

- accommodation and meals, only when participating in your course requires you to be away from home for one or more nights
- computer expenses, including interest to finance them
- depreciation of the cost of your computer, professional libraries, desks, chairs, filing cabinets, bookshelves, calculators, technical instruments, tools and other equipment (such as desk lamps)
- photocopying
- running expenses if you have a room set aside for work-related study purposes — such as the cost of heating, cooling and lighting that room while you are studying in it
- self-education expenses paid with your Overseas Study — Higher Education Loan Program (OS-HELP) loan
- stationery
- student union fees
- textbooks, professional and trade journals
- travel expenses between your home (or work) to your place of education and back
- tuition fees, including fees payable under FEE-HELP.

♀ TIP

If you have a room set aside for work-related study purposes, you can claim a fixed rate of 52 cents per hour of usage instead of keeping individual costs for heating, cooling, lighting, cleaning and decline in value of furniture.

You cannot claim a tax deduction for:

- accommodation and meals associated with day-to-day living expenses

Suzie is a manager who undertakes a self-development course consisting of the following five modules, all of equal value and cost:

- communication
- getting on with others
- handling change
- leadership
- mediation.

The module on leadership would be classed as income-related, but the remainder of the modules are private or too general in nature to be tax-deductible. As the income-related content makes up 20 per cent of the course, Suzie can only claim a deduction for 20 per cent of the costs that she incurs in undertaking the course.

29 STUDENT LOANS

There are a number of government benefits that provide financial assistance while you are studying either at university or doing a trade.

Higher Education Loan Program

University students are generally a pretty poor bunch who struggle to pay for next week's rent, let alone their course fees. So the Higher Education Loan Program (HELP) was introduced to provide a loan to assist students to pay for their university tuition.

While there is no interest rate as such, a consumer price index (CPI) adjustment is effectively charged on HELP debts on 1 June each year. According to the ATO, the average HELP debt among 2.014 million taxpayers is $20 564.

Once you start working and your income is above a minimum repayment threshold, you must make compulsory repayments, which the ATO works out via your income tax assessment, as outlined in table 3.2.

Since 1 January 2019, a combined lifetime HELP limit of $150 000 will apply to students studying medicine, dentistry and veterinary courses, reducing to $104 000 for other students.

TABLE 3.2: HELP repayment thresholds and rates (2019–20)

HELP repayment income (HRI*)	Repayment rate
Below $45 880	Nil
$45 881–$52 973	1%
$52 974–$56 151	2%
$56 152–$59 521	2.5%
$59 522–$63 092	3%
$63 093–$66 877	3.5%
$66 878–$70 890	4%
$70 891–$75 144	4.5%
$75 145–$79 652	5%
$79 653–$84 432	5.5%
$84 433–$89 498	6%
$89 499–$94 868	6.5%
$94 869–$100 560	7%
$100 561–$106 593	7.5%
$106 594–$112 989	8%
$112 990–$119 769	8.5%
$119 770–$126 955	9%
$126 956–$134 572	9.5%
$134 573 and above	10%

*HRI = taxable income plus any total net investment loss (which includes net rental losses), total reportable fringe benefits amounts, reportable super contributions and exempt foreign employment income.

Source: © Australian Taxation Office for the Commonwealth of Australia.

HECS-HELP Benefit

The HECS-HELP (Higher Education Contribution Scheme— Higher Education Loan Program) benefit was introduced on 1 July 2009 to encourage maths, science, education or nursing (including midwifery) graduates to take up employment in specified occupations. Further, it encourages early-childhood education graduates to work in specified locations including rural and regional areas, Indigenous communities and areas of socioeconomic disadvantage.

● TAX FACT

The HECS-HELP benefit is not a cash payment, but a reduction to your compulsory HELP repayment or, if you do not have to make a compulsory repayment, a reduction to your accumulated HELP debt. For the 2016–17 income year, the benefit is up to $1947.17 for early childhood education teachers, and $1825.46 for maths, science, education and nursing (including midwifery) graduates.

You may apply for the benefit each income year you are employed in an eligible occupation for a total lifetime claim of 260 weeks for each type of benefit. Claims do not have to be in consecutive years.

▲ PITFALL

The HECS-HELP Benefit has been removed since 1 June 2017 with the 2016–17 year being the last income year in which it can be claimed. However, you have two years from the end of the income year for which you are applying to submit your HECS-HELP benefit application. For example, applications for the 2016–17 income year must reach the ATO by 30 June 2019.

FEE-HELP

FEE-HELP is a loan for eligible fee-paying students enrolled at an eligible higher education provider or Open Universities of Australia.

The government has defined a limit to help pay for all or part of your tuition fees. The FEE-HELP limit, indexed each year, is the total amount available to you under both FEE-HELP and Vocational Education and

Training FEE-HELP (VET FEE-HELP). From 1 January 2019 the FEE-HELP loan limit is $104 440, except for medicine, dentistry and veterinary science courses where the limit is $150 000.

☝ TAX FACT

> There is a combined lifetime limit for all tuition fee assistance under HECS-HELP, FEE-HELP, VET FEE-HELP and VET Student Loans of $104 440 for most students increasing to $150 000 for students undertaking medicine, dentistry and veterinary science courses.

VET Student Loans

The Vocational Education and Training (VET) student loans program is an income contingent loan offered by the Government to assist eligible students undertaking certain VET diploma, advanced diploma, graduate diploma and graduate certificate courses of study at an approved VET provider.

♀ TIP

> If you take out a FEE-HELP or VET student loan to pay your tuition fees, you may be entitled to a tax deduction for the cost of your tuition fees.

OS-HELP

Overseas Study HELP (OS-HELP) is a loan that helps students meet airfares, accommodation costs and other travel expenses while undertaking some of their study overseas.

♀ TIP

> If you take out an OS-HELP loan to pay costs associated with overseas study, you may be entitled to claim a tax deduction for some of the costs.

⚠ PITFALL

> You cannot claim a tax deduction for repaying all or part of your FEE-HELP, VET student or OS-HELP loan. These loans become part of your accumulated HELP debt and are collected through the tax system once your repayment income is above the minimum repayment threshold. Voluntary and compulsory repayments are not tax-deductible.

31 SCHOLARSHIPS

How scholarships are structured will determine if they are taxable or tax-free.

Scholarships are exempt from income tax when a full-time student at a school, college or university receives a stipend for a scholarship, bursary, educational allowance or other educational assistance.

However, the principal purpose of the scholarship must be the education of the student.

Scholarship payments are exempt from income tax if:

- they are made to a full-time student at a school, college, TAFE or university
- they are made by way of scholarship, bursary, educational allowance or educational assistance
- It is accepted that selection to receive a scholarship is merit-based and that the scholarship has the requisite educational purpose.

Beware of promoters who offer to help you set up a scholarship fund to pay for your children's education with the promise that the arrangement will minimise your tax. The ATO has announced that these arrangements are not genuine scholarships as students are not independently selected on a wide range of criteria and that any scholarship payments under these arrangements are taxable in the hands of the student.

Some scholarships, bursaries, grants and awards are taxable, including education benefits provided under a friendly society scholarship plan.

Scholarship payments are subject to income tax if they are payments made:

- by the Commonwealth for education or training
- to part-time students
- under a scholarship that does not have merit-based selection
- on condition that the student will (or will if required) become an employee of the payer
- on condition that the student will (or will if required) enter into a contract with the payer that is wholly or principally for the labour of the student
- under a scholarship that is not provided principally for educational purposes.

If you are not sure about the tax consequences of a scholarship payment, contact the organisation that paid you.

> **👍 TAX FACT**
>
> If your scholarship is taxable you should advise your payer that your scholarship is assessable income—they will need to withhold tax (PAYG) from your periodic payments. You will need to show your scholarship amount as assessable income in your tax return.

> **⚠ PITFALL**
>
> If you have a family trust and distribute some of the net income to your child's school to cover their school fees then do so at your peril. The ATO views these transactions as a way to try and avoid tax and will generally assess tax on the trustees of the family trust at 47 per cent of the amount paid to the school.

32 SCHOOL BUILDING FUNDS

Many parents make payments to school building funds but they are not necessarily tax-deductible.

For a gift to a school building fund to qualify for a tax deduction, it must have the following characteristics:

- made voluntarily
- amounts to $2 or more
- made to a school building fund that is endorsed as a deductible gift recipient (DGR)
- made to a school building fund that is maintained solely for providing money for acquiring, constructing or maintaining the school or college buildings

- put towards a building, or group of buildings, used for a purpose that is connected with the curriculum of a school or college by a non-profit organisation
- does not provide a material benefit to the donor (such as a reduction in school fees, tickets to functions or the grant of scholarships to nominated students)
- essentially arises from benefaction.

The ATO will not allow deductions for building funds that are for sports grounds, tennis courts, covered play areas, car parks, landscaping, furniture or equipment. However, the ATO would allow deductions relating to the building of an indoor sports complex on school grounds (where it includes a gym, basketball court and an in-ground swimming pool) as it is a permanent structure forming an enclosure providing protection from the elements.

A multipurpose building is taken to be used as a school or college if the primary and principal use of the building (more than 50 per cent of the time) is as a school or college.

✎ EXAMPLE

A hall used by a school every weekday by students and teachers and for community meetings at weekends would qualify as a school or college building. If the hall was used as a basketball court for external groups only it would not be considered a school or college building.

Donors need to keep records of their deductible gifts for tax record-keeping purposes. Receipts for gifts must state the name of the fund, authority or institution to which the gift has been made, the DGR's Australian business number (if any) and the fact that the receipt is for a gift.

In part IV we will focus on how to maximise the tax benefits of owning a rental property as well as looking at ways to minimise any CGT liability in the future.

⚠ PITFALL

Rental properties have been on the ATO's watch list for a few years now because the sizes of the tax deductions are significant and they are a haven for errors. Each year, the ATO makes contact with many thousands of taxpayers with rental properties and asks them to explain and justify what they put in their tax return. Make sure that you can justify your claim.

Common mistakes include not having a depreciation schedule from a quantity surveyor, adding back personal usage of property, making a deduction for travel expenses and claiming capital items as repairs.

🎁 BONUS RESOURCES

For more information on how rental income and expenses are treated for tax purposes, the ATO has an excellent publication titled Rental properties (NAT 1729).

34 NEGATIVE GEARING

When expenses relating to an investment property (such as rates, insurance, repairs and interest) are greater than the rent you receive then you are negatively gearing it. The net loss is a deduction in your tax return — against other income such as salary, interest and business income — and will generally result in a refund.

👆 TAX FACT

The average net rental loss by Australian taxpayers in the 2016–17 tax year was $8771, while the average net gain for those properties positively geared was $9470.

✏ EXAMPLE

Table 4.1 is an example of how to calculate your net rental income or loss.

TABLE 4.1: net rental income or loss

	Scenario 1	Scenario 2	Scenario 3	Scenario 4
(a) Assessable income before rent	$200 000	$100 000	$70 000	$35 000
Rental income	$9300	$9300	$9300	$9300
Rental expense	$20 600	$20 600	$20 600	$20 600
(b) Net rental loss	$11 300	$11 300	$11 300	$11 300
(c) Taxable income (a − b)	$188 700	$88 700	$58 700	$23 700
(d) Marginal tax rate	47%	39%	34.5%	21%
(e) Tax benefit of negative gearing (b × d)	$5311	$4407	$3899	$2373
(f) Net cash outflow by investor (b − e)	$5989	$6893	$7401	$8927

Due to the progressive tax system in Australia, negative gearing is more beneficial to people in the higher income brackets who pay tax at

You also cannot claim interest if you:

- start using the rental property for private purposes
- use a portion of the loan for private purposes (such as purchasing a new car or investing in a super fund)
- borrow against an existing rental property to buy a new home to live in.

✏ EXAMPLE

Joe and Mary decide to take out a $290 000 loan at 4.25 per cent. $260 000 is to be used to buy a rental property and $30 000 to buy a car.

$$\text{Interest for year 1} = \$290\,000 \times 4.25\% = \$12\,325$$

Apportionment of interest payment related to rental property:

Total interest expense × (rental property loan ÷ total borrowings) = deductible interest

$$\$12\,325 \times (\$260\,000 \div \$290\,000) = \$11\,050$$

Joe and Mary can each make an interest claim of $5525 on their respective tax returns for the first year of the property.

Source: © Australian Taxation Office for the Commonwealth of Australia.

⚠ PITFALL

A common mistake is to claim a deduction for interest on the private portion of the loan. The interest expense must be apportioned between the 'deductible' and the 'private' portions of the total borrowings. The calculations can be complicated, particularly if you have a loan account that has a fluctuating balance due to a variety of deposits and withdrawals and it is used for both private purposes and rental property purposes.

If you use the equity on your existing property to buy a new house to live in, you cannot claim the interest on the additional borrowing even if you rent out the original house that the loan is secured against. Only the portion of the interest that relates to the original loan for the rental property will be deductible in this instance.

If you expect your income to be lower next year (perhaps due to maternity leave or redundancy) you should consider prepaying a year's worth of interest in advance before 30 June this year. This strategy will bring forward deductions against the higher income and thus you'll get the tax benefit back at a higher marginal rate of tax.

Don't overcommit when buying a property. Why do approximately 40 per cent of first home owners currently suffer mortgage stress? Because they purchased beyond their financial means. Make a budget before you buy. Lending organisations have been just as guilty pre-GFC in giving too much. Just because they are willing to give you $1 million doesn't mean that you have to spend it all. A minimum 20 per cent deposit will create a buffer to cater for job losses, family planning and illness, interest rate rises and unexpected costs as well as avoid mortgage insurance. Never rely on a bonus to make regular repayments. It is better to buy a smaller house and live a comfortable life with regular family holidays than have a huge house and not be able to enjoy it because you work overtime and weekends.

Can I claim all the interest on an investment property that I own with my wife as I am earning $200 000 (that is, on the highest marginal tax rate) but she is at home with the kids and doesn't earn any other income?

Nice try but unfortunately not. Any expenses for joint properties need to be apportioned to each owner based on your respective percentages of ownership. The upside is that when you sell the property and have to pay CGT down the track, your wife (assuming her income levels are still low) won't have to pay as much for her share of any gain.

36 DEPRECIATION

Behind interest, depreciation is usually the second-biggest deduction available for rental property investors, yet many don't claim it.

As your rental property gets older, the items within it experience wear and tear and they depreciate in value. The ATO allows property investors to claim a deduction for depreciation on:

* plant and equipment
* renovations or capital improvements commenced after 27 February 1992
* the building itself, if built after 18 July 1985 (and purchased before 9 May 2017 for previously used properties).

The amount of the depreciation claim can vary greatly depending on the age, use, fit-out and type of building. Plant and equipment items are basically items that can be 'easily' removed from the property as opposed to items that are permanently fixed to the structure of the building. These include things such as carpets, hot water systems, blinds and light fittings. They are usually written off over five to 10 years.

Due to the high deduction available for building costs, if you have bought an investment property that was not previously used before 9 May 2017 and it was built after 18 July 1985, it is definitely worthwhile organising a depreciation schedule from a quantity surveyor.

The ATO has a comprehensive list of more than 230 residential property items that can be depreciated.

⚠ PITFALL

Since 9 May 2017 a limit has been placed on depreciation deductions on residential rental properties to only those investors who actually purchased the plant and equipment. Subsequent owners will be unable to claim depreciation deductions on the written down value of assets purchased by previous owners.

The building write-off allowance (known as the capital works allowance) is a 2.5 per cent deduction available, written off over

40 years, for the structural element of a building including fixed, irremovable assets. It is based on historical building costs excluding the cost of all 'plant' and non-eligible items and includes things such as the bricks and mortar, walls, flooring and wiring.

There are two methods that can be applied when depreciating property for tax purposes:

- prime cost (or straight line)
- diminishing value (or reducing balance).

Under the prime cost method the deduction for each year is calculated as a percentage of the cost as follows:

cost × days owned ÷ 365
× 100% plant's effective life (in years)

Under the diminishing value method the deduction is calculated as a percentage of the balance you have left to deduct:

opening undeducted cost × days owned
÷ 365 × 200%* plant's effective life (in years)

*Note: reduce to 150% if item purchased before 10 May 2006.

The ATO specifies the individual effective life for all plant and equipment items. If you claim using the diminishing value method, you are claiming a greater proportion of the asset's cost in the earlier years. If you claim using the prime cost method, you are claiming a lower but more constant portion of the available deductions over the lifetime of the property.

The intentions of the property investor will determine which method will be most suitable for them. My experience shows that most investors employ the diminishing value method, as depreciation deductions under this method are cumulatively higher over the first five years of ownership.

39 BORROWING EXPENSES

Borrowing expenses in relation to organising a loan to purchase a rental property are tax deductions. But you can't claim them all in the first year that they are incurred, unless they are $100 or less. If your total deductible expenses are more than $100, the deduction you claim for those expenses must be spread over five years or the term of the loan, whichever is less.

> **👆 TAX FACT**
>
> If you obtained the loan part way through the income year, the deduction for the first year will be apportioned according to the number of days in the year that you had the loan.

The types of borrowing expenses you can claim as income tax deductions include the following:

- costs for preparing and filing mortgage documents
- lender's mortgage insurance
- loan establishment fees
- mortgage broker fees

- stamp duty charged on your mortgage
- title search fees charged by your lender
- valuation fees required for loan approval.

Mortgage discharge expenses, including those ridiculously high penalty interest costs involved in discharging a fixed-rate mortgage, are deductible in the year they are incurred to the extent that you took out the mortgage as security for the repayment of money you borrowed to use to produce assessable income.

⚠ PITFALL

The following cannot be claimed as borrowing expenses:

- stamp duty charged by your state/territory government on the transfer (purchase) of the property title—this stamp duty can be included in calculating the 'cost base' of your property for CGT purposes
- insurance premiums where under the policy your loan will be paid out in the event that you die or become disabled or unemployed (this is a private expense)
- borrowing expenses on the portion of the loan you use for private purposes (for example, money used to buy a boat).

♀ TIP

Stamp duty, preparation and registration costs you incur on the lease of an Australian Capital Territory (ACT) property are deductible to the extent that you use the property as a rental property. This is because freehold title cannot be obtained for properties in the ACT. They are commonly acquired under a 99-year Crown lease.

✎ EXAMPLE

On 16 September 2019, Robert took out a 30-year loan of $450 000 to purchase a rental property. Robert's deductible expenses were:

- $950 stamp duty on the mortgage
- $650 loan establishment fees
- $250 valuation fees required for loan.

41 OTHER RENTAL PROPERTY DEDUCTIONS

You may be entitled to claim an immediate deduction on these other property expenses in the income year you incur the expense:

- advertising for tenants
- bank charges
- body corporate fees and charges, also known as strata levies
- cleaning
- council rates
- electricity and gas
- gardening and lawnmowing
- in-house audio/video service charges
- insurance (building, contents and public liability)
- land tax
- letting fees
- pest control
- property agent's fees and commission
- quantity surveyor's fees
- secretarial and bookkeeping fees
- security patrol fees
- servicing costs — for example, servicing a water heater
- stationery and postage
- tax-related expenses
- telephone calls and rental
- water rates.

You can claim a deduction for these expenses only if you actually incur them and they are not paid by the tenant.

Land tax is a state tax imposed by each Australian state and territory (except the Northern Territory) and, as you might expect, each state has a different set of rules including different rates, thresholds and due dates. It is calculated on the unimproved value of the land (rather than the whole property value).

The tax is generally levied on the owners of land at midnight on 31 December of each year in New South Wales and Victoria (and 30 June for most other states) for land values greater than the threshold level, which are outlined in table 4.3. If you are liable for land tax you need to submit a land tax return. Owner-occupied homes or land used for primary production are generally exempt from land tax, while properties held in a trust or company generally have a zero threshold.

♀ TIP

While it may not be tax deductible, take out basic life insurance that will cover your mortgage so that you have peace of mind knowing that your loved ones are not forced to sell when you (and your income) are no longer around.

TABLE 4.3: state land tax thresholds

State	Land tax threshold	Website
ACT	$0	www.revenue.act.gov.au
NSW	$692 000	www.osr.nsw.gov.au
Qld	$600 000	www.osr.qld.gov.au
SA	$369 000	www.revenuesa.sa.gov.au
Tas.	$25 000	www.sro.tas.gov.au
Vic.	$250 000	www.sro.vic.gov.au
WA	$300 000	www.osr.wa.gov.au

You can claim a deduction for certain expenses you incur for the period your property is rented or is available for rent. However, you cannot claim expenses of a capital nature or private nature — although you may be able to claim decline-in-value deductions or capital works deductions for certain capital expenses or include certain capital costs in the cost base of the property for CGT purposes.

⚠ PITFALL

Expenses for which the ATO will not allow you to claim include:

- acquisition and disposal costs of the property
- body corporate payments to a special-purpose fund to pay for particular capital expenditure
- expenses you do not actually incur, such as water or electricity charges paid by your tenants
- expenses that are not related to the rental of a property, such as expenses connected to your own use of a holiday home that you rent out for part of the year
- travel in relation to inspecting, maintaining or collecting rent for a residential rental property.

♀ TIP

Make sure you have receipts to justify the deductions you are claiming, and can justify the connection between the expense and deriving the rental income (for example, it wasn't also for a private purpose).

42 FOREIGN INVESTMENT PROPERTIES

Australian tax residents have always been required to pay tax on their worldwide income. This includes declaring income earned from an overseas property that you may own in your Australian income tax return — even if it has been, or will be, taxed outside Australia.

You can also claim the deductions (such as interest, repairs, depreciation, rates and insurance) as mentioned in tips 35–41 for a foreign rental property.

If your overseas property tax deductions are greater than your overseas rental income, you will have a foreign income loss. For many years, these foreign losses were quarantined and had to be carried forward to future years and only be offset against future foreign income.

However, many foreign property investors are not aware of the change in the rules a few years ago. Since 1 July 2008, foreign losses have not been quarantined from domestic income. This means that you can now 'negatively gear' your foreign income loss to reduce your Australian income.

⚠ PITFALL

From 9 May 2017, an annual vacancy fee of at least $5500 applies to foreign owners who leave their Australian properties unoccupied or not available for rent for 6 months or more each year. The fee increases for properties valued above $1 million. The fee is paid via an annual return which can be found here www.ato.gov.au/FIRBvacancyfee/.

Before you calculate your net income, all foreign income, deductions and foreign tax paid must be converted to Australian dollars. There are two ways of doing this. Depending on your circumstances, you can use:

- the exchange rates prevailing at specific times (generally used for specific transactions such as monthly rent, asset purchases and one-off expenses such as rates and insurance)
- an average exchange rate (generally used for expenses incurred over a period such as loan interest).

While a person's principal place of residence is CGT-free when they sell it, it is possible to move out of the property, rent it and still claim this exemption for up to six years. After that time, the CGT clock is no longer frozen and starts ticking

🎁 BONUS RESOURCES

For more information about CGT, the ATO has the excellent *Personal investors guide to capital gains tax* (NAT 4152).

📢 PROPOSED CHANGE

From 1 January 2018, investment properties which are supplied for at least three years via Community Housing Providers as affordable housing will be eligible for an additional 10 per cent CGT discount.

? FAQ

If we move into the granny flat in the back of our property and rent out the main house, are we subject to capital gains tax?

When you move into your granny flat, it will be treated as a separate asset for CGT purposes. You will need to consider on which asset to claim the principal place of residence exemption—ideally the property with the greatest opportunity for growth, which will probably be the main house. Of course, any periods that you live in both places at the same time are exempt from CGT.

44 PAYG WITHHOLDING VARIATION

As mentioned earlier, one of the major downsides to negative gearing is cash flow.

My preference is that you wait until the end of the year to get your refund as it is a forced form of saving. But if cash flow is tight, you may want to complete a pay-as-you-go (PAYG) withholding variation application, which reduces the tax from your monthly pay. The form is virtually a mini tax return which estimates your taxable income. You still need to lodge an annual tax return.

✐ EXAMPLE

Jason is on the highest marginal tax rate. In the year ending 30 June 2020 he expects to incur a net rental loss of $20 000. Instead of waiting to lodge his 2019–20 tax return in July 2020 and getting a refund of $9400, he can submit a PAYG withholding variation application with the ATO in May 2019. As a result, Jason has $816.67 less PAYG tax withheld from his salary each month to help him meet his mortgage commitments instead of waiting until the end of the financial year.

♀ TIP

The rate of withholding will hopefully match your year-end tax liability. If you underestimate your income then expect to have a tax shortfall, which isn't desirable. Instead, make sure you give yourself a buffer by not being too aggressive with estimating deductions.

If your circumstances change after your PAYG variation is approved (perhaps you increased the rent, your expenses are lower than expected or you sold your property), then submit a new PAYG variation straight away. Otherwise you may have an unwanted tax liability at the end of the year.

You can lodge your application in paper form or electronically over the internet. The varied rate of withholding will start from the next payday after your pay office receives the notice of withholding variation approval from the ATO.

♠ TAX FACT

PAYG withholding variations are not solely available to taxpayers who are negatively gearing rental properties. They can also be used for other purposes where a taxpayer's assessable income is substantially reduced for tax-deductible expenditure such as work-related car expenses, self-education costs or margin-loan interest.

Your variation generally finishes on 30 June each year so you need to do a new PAYG withholding variation application each year—they do not roll forward. To continue to have reduced tax withheld after this date, you must lodge another PAYG withholding variation application at least six weeks beforehand; that is, by 15 May each year.

Anyone using the withholding variation strategy to help with cash flow needs to be disciplined enough to use the extra money to meet the shortfall, rather than using it for everyday living expenses.

Remember, if you apply for advanced refunds in this way, there will be no end-of-year tax deduction and no 'forced form of saving'.

🎁 BONUS RESOURCES

If you believe your circumstances warrant a reduction to your rate or amount of withholding, you can apply to the ATO for a variation using the PAYG withholding variation application (NAT 2036).

45 PROPERTY GENUINELY AVAILABLE FOR RENT

As we have seen, deductions for investment properties can be quite substantial and generate large tax refunds, particularly if a property doesn't generate much rent by comparison. However, the property must be rented, or 'genuinely available' for rental, in the income year for which you claim a deduction. If you start to use the property for private purposes, you cannot claim any interest expenses you incur after you start using the property for private purposes.

💡 TIP

It is very important that you have a clear intention of renting your property. If you make no attempt to advertise your property or set the rent unrealistically high, the ATO will find that you have no intention of renting your property and your rental claims may not be allowed.

In some situations, rental expenses may need to be apportioned. For example, if your holiday home is used by you, your friends or your relatives free of charge for part of the year, you are not entitled to a deduction for costs incurred during those periods.

The 2017–18 federal budget has proposed that foreign residents will no longer be able to claim the main residence CGT exemption.

👍 TAX FACT

If you rent your property to family or friends at below market rent, the ATO may treat this as a 'private' arrangement and only allow you to claim sufficient deductions to offset the rent, but not enough to make a tax loss.

⚠ PITFALL

Be careful not to overstate interest deductions where the loan is partly for private purposes, such as claiming interest on a holiday house property where it is used, say for one month (one-twelfth), by your family for holidays.

🎁 BONUS RESOURCES

For more information about tax and shares, the ATO has an excellent publication called *You and your shares 2018* (NAT 2632).

46 DIVIDENDS

Being a shareholder entitles you to a share of a company's profits that are usually paid as dividends. In Australia, there are two types of dividends that are assessable for tax purposes:

* franked dividends
* unfranked dividends.

⚠ PITFALL

According to the ATO, if a private company lends money to a shareholder (or associate) and the loan is not fully repaid before the end of the income year, the outstanding amount may be treated as a non-commercial loan and assessed as an unfranked dividend in the shareholder's tax return to the extent of the private company's retained earnings.

Franked dividends are dividends paid by Australian companies from profits that have been taxed previously. A dividend which carries tax credits for the whole dividend is known as a fully franked dividend.

Unfranked dividends are dividends paid by Australian companies from profits that have not had any company tax paid on them.

♠ TAX FACT

Franked dividends paid to non-resident individuals are exempt from Australian income tax. However, they are not entitled to any franking tax offset for franked dividends.

Any unfranked dividends paid to a non-resident are subject to a final withholding tax, generally 15 per cent if Australia has a double taxation agreement with the taxpayer's resident country, otherwise at 30 per cent.

When an Australian company pays you a dividend, it must also send you a statement advising:

- the amount of the dividend that is unfranked
- the amount of the dividend that is franked
- any franking credits
- any TFN withholding tax withheld on unfranked dividends.

♀ TIP

Make sure you quote your TFN to any company that pays you a dividend, otherwise withholding tax at the highest marginal rate (47 per cent) will be deducted on any unfranked dividends paid to you. If you have TFN tax withheld you must include it in your tax return so that you receive the credit in your assessment.

✏ EXAMPLE

This is an example of what a dividend statement would look like:

ADC Limited

ABN 12 345 678 901

Shareholder dividend statement

Payment date 15 February 2020

Notification of 2019 final dividend — paid 15 February 2020

Security description	No. of shares	Unfranked amount	Franked amount	Franking credit
Ordinary shares	18 000	$500	$700	$300
TFN amount	$0.00			
Net dividend	$1200.00			

Please note that your tax file number has been received and recorded.

Please retain this advice for taxation purposes.

Please advise promptly in writing of any change of address.

Source: © Australian Taxation Office for the Commonwealth of Australia.

♀ TIP

Taxpayers regularly get the timing of the dividend payments wrong. Only dividends paid between 1 July and 30 June the following year should be included in your return. Confusion usually occurs when a final dividend is paid in July or August yet the dividend statement says that it is in respect of the year ended 30 June. In this instance the dividend should be declared in the following tax year.

👍 TAX FACT

If you had any shares in joint names, you are not required to lodge a separate partnership tax return. Simply show your proportion of any dividends paid in your individual tax return.

47 FRANKING CREDITS

Franking credits, also known as imputation credits, were introduced in 1985 to prevent the double taxation of dividends to individual shareholders after companies had already paid tax on the profits distributed.

Franking credits are amounts of tax paid by the company that are allocated to your franked dividend. There is no franking credit associated with an unfranked dividend.

👆 TAX FACT

Dividends paid to shareholders by Australian companies are taxed under an 'imputation' system where tax paid by a company may be imputed to shareholders. Any tax paid by the company is allocated by way of franking credits attached to the dividends paid to shareholders.

The amount of the franking credit is calculated as follows:

Franking credit = franked dividend paid × company

tax rate ÷ (100% − company tax rate)

The company tax rate for businesses with turnover greater than $50 million is 30 per cent, but reduces to 27.5 per cent for small/medium companies under this threshold. So if you receive a dividend from a public company, you calculate the franking credit as follows:

Franking credit = franked dividend × 30 ÷ 70

✏️ EXAMPLE

On 15 February 2020 an Australian resident company, ABC Ltd, paid Peter, a resident individual, a fully franked dividend of $700 and an unfranked dividend of $500.

Peter's assessable income for 2019–20 in respect of the dividend is:

Unfranked dividend	$500
Franked dividend	$700
Franking credit ($700 × 30 ÷ 70)	$300
Total assessable dividends	**$1500**

A lot of people think that because they didn't receive a dividend in cash, but rather received some more shares in the company via a DRP, the dividend is not taxable. This is incorrect. All dividends paid, whether in cash or shares, must be included in your assessable income in the year they are received.

You are also subject to tax on any capital gain made when you dispose of shares you have received under a DRP. For the purpose of calculating any capital gain or loss, the cost of the shares acquired under a DRP is taken as the market price on the date of the dividend as shown on the statement.

♀ TIP

Keep a record of all reinvested dividends to help you work out any capital gains or losses you make when you dispose of shares. The cost base must be the same as the amount that you previously declared as a dividend.

👍 TAX FACT

In addition to DRPs, shareholders may receive bonus shares in a company from time to time which are extra shares received based on your existing shareholding. They are not taxable on receipt but if you dispose of any bonus shares received after 19 September 1985 you may have to:

- pay tax on any capital gain
- average out the cost base of your existing shares in the company.

49 SHARES OWNED BY LOW INCOME EARNERS

There can be some significant benefits in holding shares in the name of the spouse who is on the lower income, because any dividends (and capital gains) are taxed at a lower rate.

The marginal income tax rates for resident individuals for the 2019–20 financial year are shown in table 5.1.

TABLE 5.1: tax rates for individuals excluding levies 2019–20

Taxable income	Tax on this income
0–$18 200	Nil
$18 201–$37 000	19c for each $1 over $18 200
$37 001–$90 000	$3572 plus 32.5c for each $1 over $37 000
$90 001–$180 000	$20 797 plus 37c for each $1 over $90 000
$180 001 and over	$54 097 plus 45c for each $1 over $180 000

Source: © Australian Taxation Office for the Commonwealth of Australia.

💡 TIP

For those earning less than $90 000, franked dividends are almost tax-free because they get a credit for the 30 per cent company tax already paid — similar to the marginal rate at that level.

For those on lower marginal tax rates (that is, earning less than $37 000), the excess franking tax offsets can be used to reduce your tax liability from other forms of income, including net taxable capital gains, or can even be refunded.

✏️ EXAMPLE

Tom earns $310 000 while his wife Suzie earns $20 000. They just sold their house and are considering purchasing a share portfolio of stocks in blue-chip companies. As Suzie has a marginal tax rate of 21 per cent (including the 2 per cent Medicare levy), it is more beneficial for her to own the portfolio in her name than for Tom to own it, as he is in the highest tax bracket of 47 per cent.

The tax savings on a share portfolio in Suzie's name that generates an annual income stream of franked dividends of, say, $20 000 would be as much as $4590, or 22.9% per cent of the income received.

⚠ PITFALL

A share portfolio in the low-income-earning spouse's name may have an impact on any government benefits being received, as dividend income and capital gains are included under the income test and the share portfolio itself is assessed by Centrelink under its assets test.

If there are some significant capital gains in a portfolio, then they may push the low-income earner into a higher tax bracket, thus negating some of the tax benefits that may be received. In this instance it may be an idea to spread the disposal over a few income years.

There is also a need to look into a crystal ball and forecast what income levels will be for spouses in future years, especially if the current income is abnormally low, and that events such as returning to work after the kids go back to school are fully considered prior to making any purchase.

✎ EXAMPLE

If, in two years' time, Suzie gets a full-time job with a salary of $180 000 and Tom decides to reduce the number of days he works and only earns $60 000 per annum, there is no longer any benefit in having the share portfolio in Suzie's name as she is now in a high tax bracket of 47 per cent while Tom only pays 34.5 per cent.

While it is possible to transfer shares across to the other partner's name in an off-market transfer, such an event would trigger CGT, which might negate any benefit gained by such a switch.

♀ TIP

Senior Australians are not required to pay any income tax if their income is below $32 279 for singles (or $28 974 each if a couple). As a result, notwithstanding the risks associated with share-price fluctuations, an investment strategy of having a share portfolio that generates fully franked dividends (and franking credits subsequently refunded) may be quite lucrative for those eligible for the senior and pensioner tax offset.

50 BORROWING TO BUY SHARES

A common, yet risky, investment strategy used by share investors has been to borrow money, usually via a margin loan, to buy shares.

⚠ PITFALL

Borrowing is a good strategy in a rising market, but it can multiply any losses in a falling market. The last thing you want is a loan to repay but no shares to show for it. Don't consider borrowing if you are new to investing.

Just like the tax rules for investment properties, if you borrow money to buy a share portfolio, you can claim a tax deduction for the loan interest, provided it is reasonable to expect that assessable income (dividends or capital gains) will be derived from the share investment. If the loan has a private component, you will only be able to claim interest incurred on the part of the loan used to acquire the shares.

The benefit of such a strategy is that the interest expense should offset any dividend income received, resulting in franking credits that can be offset against other taxable income. Hopefully the shares increase in value under this strategy and any capital gains are only realised in a later year when the taxpayer is on a lower tax rate, for example, in retirement.

♀ TIP

If you expect to earn a lower income next tax year (for example, due to redundancy or maternity leave), an excellent strategy to consider is prepaying interest 12 months in advance before year end on your margin loan to maximise your tax deduction based on the higher marginal tax rate.

Other deductions

Any other expenses you incur that relate directly to maintaining your portfolio are also deductible, including:

- bookkeeping expenses
- telephone
- postage.

52 CAPITAL GAINS TAX ON SHARES

With a potential to go up to 47 per cent, CGT can have a hugely negative impact when calculating the net return on an investment. It is a tax imposed upon gains made from the disposal of assets, usually shares or investment properties, that were acquired after 19 September 1985. When a net capital gain arises it is included in your taxable income and is subject to income tax at the marginal tax rates.

You make a capital gain or loss when a 'CGT event' occurs. These events could be when you:

- sell your shares
- have your shares redeemed, cancelled, surrendered or considered valueless by a liquidator
- receive a payment (other than dividends) from a company as a shareholder
- give away your shares

The capital gain is calculated on the difference between the proceeds that you receive from the sale of your shares and the amount you originally paid for them. Brokerage is included in your cost base.

> **♀ TIP**
>
> The simplest way to reduce CGT is to hold onto the investment for more than 12 months. Since September 1999, a 50 per cent discount on capital gains is allowed for shares held for longer than a year.

> **▲ PITFALL**
>
> If you do try to wait for the 12 months' holding period to tick over, be careful that the sharemarket doesn't collapse during this time. A dramatic fall in share price could erase any tax benefit that the 50 per cent discount provides if you are not careful.

Shares sold back to a company under a buyback arrangement result in a capital gain or loss. Part of the buyback price may be treated as an assessable dividend for income tax purposes. If the buyback comes from a listed company, a class ruling is usually issued to assist shareholders with any tax implications.

To calculate any capital gain, the ATO requires you to keep proper records for tax purposes including:

- 'buy' and 'sell' contract notes, showing the date and amounts
- dividend statements for any dividend reinvestment schemes that you participated in.

The ATO will allow you to establish a CGT asset register (but only if it is in a certain format) if you do not want to keep your records, particularly if you hold shares for a long time. For more information, see the ATO's Taxation Ruling TR 2002/10 Income tax: capital gains tax: asset register.

TIP

Since 1 July 2016, investment in a qualifying early stage innovation company (ESIC) by sophisticated investors, may result in a number of tax incentives including:

- 20 per cent non-refundable carry forward tax offset on the amount paid for the investment, capped at $200 000 per annum
- no tax on capital gains realised on qualifying shares in an ESIC held between 12 months and less than ten years.

The incentives are not available to those who are not sophisticated investors and whose total investment in an income year is more than $50 000.

BONUS RESOURCES

For more information about CGT, the ATO has the excellent *Personal investors guide to capital gains tax* (NAT 4152).

53 REALISING CAPITAL LOSSES

One of the best ways to reduce your CGT bill is to offset any gains that you have made during the financial year with any losses incurred on other share investments. It is important to note that the losses must be crystallised (or realised) in order for them to be offset against any capital gains made. If a loss remains unrealised (not sold) at the end of the financial year, you cannot claim it in your return until the year that you actually dispose of the investment.

✏ EXAMPLE

Peter makes a $6200 capital gain on the sale of BHP shares in July 2019. He also owns shares in another stock, XYZ, which he bought for $10 000 but which are now only worth $4000. If he realises this loss by selling these shares before 30 June 2020 he can reduce his taxable capital gain by $6000 to only $200. If Peter disposes of these XYZ shares after 1 July 2020, then he must pay tax on the whole $6200 gain.

It is good tax-planning practice to see if there is an opportunity to reduce the tax on gains made earlier in the year by selling a few non-performing shares. This is particularly relevant if the sharemarket is performing like a roller-coaster and there is a slump after a big rise earlier in the year.

♀ TIP

Maintain an Excel spreadsheet to keep track of the cost base and market value of your share portfolio on a stock-by-stock basis. This will assist with the tax-planning process to help determine which stocks could be sold to offset capital gains already made during the year.

Obviously, if you haven't made any gains in the year then there is no need to crystallise any losses that you are currently carrying in your share portfolio.

♀ TIP

Realised capital losses can be carried forward indefinitely until they are fully utilised. Check your past tax returns for any available from previous years.

While you could purchase back your shares that have been realised for the loss, it is not advisable. Although yet to be challenged in the courts, the ATO has warned that the practice of 'wash sales' (where

👍 TAX FACT

Often family members give shares to relatives while they are still alive; for example, a parent gives shares to their child. If you receive shares as a gift, the market value on the date that you received them will be your cost base for CGT purposes.

55 SHARE TRADERS VERSUS SHARE INVESTORS

The distinction between share traders and share investors is significant for tax purposes as you deal with gains and losses differently.

The ATO will consider you to be a share trader if you conduct your business activities for the sole purpose of earning income from the buying and selling of shares. Losses incurred are treated the same as any other losses from business—provided the non–commercial losses rules are satisfied, an immediate deduction is available against other taxable income.

👍 TAX FACT

In financial years when shares plummet, it is quite common for taxpayers to try to class themselves as share traders.

To be classed as a share trader, the ATO may ask you to prove you are carrying on a share trading business, including providing evidence that shows:

- the purchase and sale of shares on a regular basis
- the use of any share trading techniques
- decisions based on thorough analysis of relevant market information
- a contingency plan in the event of a major market shift
- a trading plan showing analysis and research of each potential investment and the market, and any formula for deciding when to hold or sell investments.

The ATO will consider you to be a share investor if you:

- invest in shares with the sole intention of earning income from dividends and capital growth
- are eligible for the 50 per cent CGT discount on gain
- claim losses incurred as a capital loss and not as an immediate deduction
- carry forward capital losses to be offset against future capital gains.

In financial years when shares rocket up, it is quite common for taxpayers to try to class themselves as share investors so they can get the 50 per cent CGT discount on gains made for shares held for more than 12 months.

How you treat your investment activities in prior tax returns is the main factor in determining the correct way to deal with losses in the current tax year. If there has been little or no change in your investment activity, you should treat the investments in the same manner again in the current year.

✎ EXAMPLE

George has been purchasing shares for a number of years for the purpose of earning income from dividends. In a previous year George sold shares and claimed the 50 per cent CGT discount. It is expected that George will claim any losses in the current year as capital losses.

If you change from being a share investor to being a share trader (or vice versa) the ATO may request evidence that proves the change is accurate and that you have not declared your income incorrectly in previous tax returns.

⚠ PITFALL

The ATO has issued a warning to taxpayers who seek to change their status from that of a share investor to a share trader. For more information, see *Taxpayer Alert 2009/12*.

If an ATO audit finds that you have incorrectly claimed trading losses and you are unable to satisfactorily show that you are carrying on an investment business, your deduction will be disallowed and penalties may apply.

56 RIGHTS AND OPTIONS

Companies sometimes issue their shareholders with rights or options to purchase additional shares.

A 'one-for-ten' rights issue means that shareholders are entitled to purchase an additional share for every 10 shares that they own. The right can be exercised, sold on the stock exchange or simply allowed to lapse.

Where the above criteria are satisfied then the only tax consequences that may arise with rights issues involve CGT. In other situations, rights issues may result in having to disclose assessable income in your tax return.

If you are issued a right to sell your shares (that is, a put), then the market value of the right should be included in your assessable income at the time of issue and will form part of your cost base for the rights or shares, if you exercised the rights.

Companies may also issue their shareholders with options. If you receive an option, you have the right to acquire or sell shares in the company at a specified price on a specified date. These options can be traded on the stock exchange or allowed to lapse.

Exchange-traded options are types of options that are not created by the company but by independent third parties and are traded on the stock exchange. Option trading will generally be considered a business activity and subject to the normal business income rules.

If you have a share portfolio in your own name and the sharemarket crashes, you have a great opportunity. If you are confident that the shares will bounce back, transfer the shares 'in-specie' into a lower taxed environment of an SMSF. The SMSF will potentially only pay 10 per cent tax on future gains and can use excess franking credits on other income under this strategy.

However, the 'in-specie transfer' will be considered a CGT event and will trigger the CGT provisions for the individual taxpayer. To limit any CGT it is preferable to transfer shares that have not incurred large gains or those that can be offset against other capital losses.

59 CRYPTOCURRENCY

It's amazing how the financial world evolves. When I wrote the first edition of this book in 2011 I would have been more likely to write about kryptonite and its impact on super rather than cryptocurrency.

Bitcoin. Ethereum. Litecoin. Blockchain. Ripple. EOS. The cryptocurrency (or altcoin) list seems to get added to almost by the week. Okay I will admit, I hardly know anything about them. But as they are digital assets which people invest or trade in then we do need to worry about their treatment for taxation purposes.

The ATO's interpretation on the tax treatment of cryptocurrency is slowly evolving as transactions in cryptocurrency become more and more common. Although it does vary from crypto to crypto, the ATO's view is that they are neither 'money' nor 'currency' but rather 'property' and are assets which are taxable under CGT regulations.

A CGT event occurs when you dispose of your cryptocurrency. If you make a capital gain on the disposal of a cryptocurrency, some or all of the gain may be taxed. Certain capital gains or losses that arise from the disposal of cryptocurrency that is a personal use asset may be disregarded.

Only capital gains you make from personal use assets acquired for more than $10 000 are taxable for CGT purposes. However, all capital losses you make on personal use assets are disregarded.

Cryptocurrency is not a personal use asset if it is acquired, kept or used:

- as an investment
- in a profit–making scheme
- in the course of carrying on a business.

PART VI

YOUR SUPERANNUATION

Superannuation is money set aside throughout your working life to provide for your retirement. Behind the family home, it's the second-largest asset for many Australians, maybe even the largest. But it is ridiculous how little attention is paid to it. You need to take the time to look after one of your biggest assets. It doesn't need much. If you don't have enough money in super to look after yourself when you retire there are government pensions to support you.

> **👍 TAX FACT**
>
> As at 31 December 2018, the total assets within Australian superannuation were $2.653 trillion (Australian Prudential Regulation Authority 2019b), which was greater than the market capitalisation of the Australian equities market of $1.790 trillion (Australian Securities Exchange 2019), the combined deposits on the books of all Australian banks of $2.179 trillion (Australian Prudential Regulation Authority 2019a) and the Gross Domestic Product of Australia of $1.894 trillion (Australian Bureau of Statistics 2019).

Figure 6.1 reports the movement in total assets held by the various segments of the Australian superannuation industry since 1996. Total assets in the industry have increased by 1081 per cent from $245.5 billion to $2653.2 billion as at 31 December 2018, the number of funds rising almost sixfold from 105 377 in 1996 to 599 032 funds and the number of member accounts doubling during the period to approximately 32 million (Australian Prudential Regulation Authority 2019b). The economic significance of the superannuation industry in Australia, measured by assets in the industry as a proportion of GDP, has jumped from 37.9 per cent in 1996 to 140.1 per cent in December 2018 (Australian Bureau of Statistics 2019). A notable feature of figure 6.1 is the rapid growth of the SMSF sector over the past decade, which now comprises the largest segment of the superannuation industry (by number of funds and assets). Funds under management in the SMSF sector have risen from $60.9 billion (330 000 members in 166 475 funds) in 1999/2000 to $726.5 billion (1 127 304 members in 597 009 funds) in December 2018 (Australian Taxation Office 2019). SMSFs now account for 27.38 per cent of assets in the Australian pension industry and 99.66 per cent of funds, compared with 43.17 per cent and 0.01 per cent for not-for-profit (corporate plus public sector plus industry) funds and 22.2 per cent and 0.02 per cent for retail funds.

FIGURE 6.1: superannuation industry in Australia 1996–2015 by total assets ($ billion)

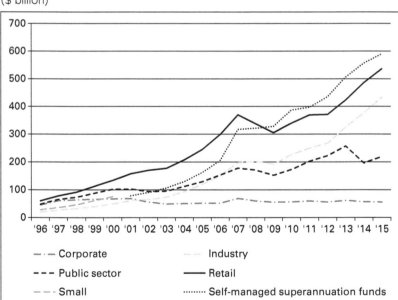

Sources: Arnold et al. (2015), Bird et al. (2018), Raftery (2014)

It is never too late to start putting money into super, but the earlier you can start the better because small amounts added when you are young can make a big difference to the size of your savings in retirement.

Super funds can invest in shares, property, term deposits and managed funds and they enjoy very generous tax concessions, with complying super funds receiving more favourable tax treatment than companies and individuals earning over $18 200.

👆 TAX FACT

The tax rate for a complying superannuation fund on its net income and contributions is 15 per cent. Contributions are taxed at 30 per cent if they are for individuals with income greater than $250 000. Capital gains tax is reduced to 10 per cent when assets are held for at least one year.

Part VI will focus on different ways to give your super a boost and how to access it in the most tax-effective way.

⚠ PITFALL

Before you roll over monies into a new super fund, check to see if you have an insurance policy attached to your existing fund. People with longstanding insurance cover will need to renew it if they move into an SMSF, and may fail new conditions such as declaring pre-existing conditions. Ask your old fund if there is a 'continuation option' that will allow you to buy a private policy without having to provide medical evidence.

💡 TIP

If you start a new job, chances are that you are earning more than your previous role. How about using some of that money to make extra contributions to superannuation via salary sacrifice? The sooner you start saving, the bigger your retirement kitty will be.

♀ TIP

If you are under 65 years old for at least one day of the financial year and your superannuation balance is no more than $1.4 million, you can bring forward two years' worth of contributions, giving you a maximum non-concessional contributions cap of $300 000 in the current year (with nothing in the following two years if the whole amount is contributed in the first year of the period), rather than a $100 000 cap in each of the three years. Table 6.1 shows that the maximum non-concessional cap that you can bring forward reduces when superannuation balances are over $1.4 million. The period begins in the first year that you contribute more than the non-concessional contribution cap.

TABLE 6.1: non-concessional contribution limits under bring forward period rule (2019–20)

Total superannuation balance prior year	Maximum non-concessional contribution cap	Bring-forward period
< $1 400 000	$300 000	3 years
$1 400 000–$1 499 999	$200 000	2 years
$1 500 000–$1 599 999	$100 000	nil
> $1 600 000	nil	nil

Source: © Australian Taxation Office for the Commonwealth of Australia.

If you triggered the three year bring forward period in 2016–17 financial year (when the non-concessional cap limit was $180 000), the maximum non-concessional contribution cap in 2018–19 will be $380 000. Since 1 July 2018, if you are aged 65 and over and you sell your family home of at least ten years, you can make a non-concessional contribution of up to $300 000 regardless of how much super you have.

♠ TAX FACT

The date that your super fund receives your contributions can also be important as contributions are counted towards the caps in the year in which they are received and credited by your super fund. A cheque sent at the end of June but not received by the super fund until July will count towards the next financial year's cap.

Any amount over the concessional contributions cap will be taxed at an additional 32 per cent while any amount over the non-concessional cap attracts 47 per cent tax. You're liable for this tax, but you can use a release authority from the ATO to access your super fund monies to pay the amount.

Excess concessional contributions are included in an individual's taxable income and taxed at their marginal tax rate (plus an interest charge) regardless of their income or the cause of the breach. The individual can choose to pay the tax bill from their own sources, or use their after-tax excess concessional contribution from super. An excess contribution charge (currently 4.94 per cent) is applied to the additional income tax arising due to excess concessional contributions included in your income tax return.

61 TRANSFER BALANCE CAP

Anyone who knows me will tell you that I have been harping on for years about how superannuation is one of the very best places to save money on your tax legally especially with no tax to pay on your savings in retirement mode. Unfortunately, a few took full advantage of the generous loophole by placing millions upon millions into super to avoid paying any tax at all. So it came as no surprise that the regulators tried to limit this loophole by placing a cap from 1 July 2017 on how much super you can have in retirement without paying tax.

The transfer balance cap is a limit — currently $1.6 million — on how much superannuation can be transferred from your accumulation super account to a tax-free 'retirement phase' account. It will be indexed to CPI, rounded down to the nearest $100 000. All your account balances are included when working out this amount. It does not matter how many accounts you hold these balances in.

⚠ PITFALL

Since 1 July 2017 the tax-free status of retirement accounts are restricted with a transfer balance cap of $1.6 million on amounts moving into tax-free pension phase. Balances are able to increase above this cap based on growth of tax-free earnings (after minimum withdrawals). Amounts above $1.6 million as at 1 July 2017 (or subsequent date that the transfer balance account is created) must be either taken as a lump sum (available for those over preservation age) or rolled into an accumulation fund with subsequent earnings taxed at 15 per cent.

If you exceed your transfer balance cap, you may have to convert a portion of your retirement phase income stream into a lump sum accumulation account and pay tax on the notional earnings related to that excess. It still remains an attractive concession with the tax rate only being 15 per cent on the excess with earnings on the first $1.6 million (or $3.2 million for couples) being tax-free.

⚠ PITFALL

When the amount in your retirement phase account grows over time (through investment earnings) to more than $1.6 million, you won't exceed your cap. You can continue to make multiple transfers into the retirement phase as long as you remain below the cap. However, if the amount in your retirement phase account goes down over time, you cannot top it up if you have already used all of your $1.6 million cap space.

✋ TAX FACT

The super co-contribution is only available to those with a total superannuation balance of less than $1 600 000 at the end of the previous financial year.

The imposition of the $1.6 million transfer balance cap means that some assets which exceed the cap will need to be moved from pension mode back into accumulation mode. If an SMSF uses the segregation of assets method, then moving assets back into accumulation mode could provide the opportunity for the SMSF to keep assets that might incur a capital gains tax liability in pension mode whilst transferring assets which are unlikely to incur a capital gains tax liability – or will produce lower income (for example cash and fixed interest investments) – back into accumulation mode

With a $1.6 million transfer balance cap on superannuation that came into effect 1 July 2017, there is an opportunity to split superannuation contributions between spouses such that each spouse maximises their respective $1.6 million thresholds (that is, $3.2 million in total) before they retire.

If you have an excess transfer balance it is important to transfer the money from retirement phase as soon as possible to limit the amount of excess transfer balance tax payable. The tax payable is determined by calculating daily notional earnings based on the General Interest Charge rate (currently 8.96 per cent). The tax rate is 15 per cent for the first time you have an excess transfer balance which doubles to 30 per cent if you go over the transfer balance cap again.

Since 1 July 2017 the use of limited recourse borrowing arrangements are included in a member's total superannuation and $1.6 million transfer balance cap calculations.

Although a downsizer contribution needs to be made within 90 days of receiving the proceeds of sale, the ATO will allow you to apply for a longer period if required because of circumstances outside your control. The request should be made within the initial 90-day timeframe and it will usually be granted due to ill health, a death in the family, or moving house.

It is possible to make multiple downsizer contributions but they must all come from the proceeds of a single sale and the total of all your contributions must not exceed $300 000 or the total proceeds of the sale less any other downsizer contributions that have been made by your spouse.

A Downsizer contribution into super form needs to be submitted to your superannuation fund by the time you make your contribution. False and misleading penalties may be applied if the ATO subsequently determines that your downsizer contribution was not eligible. In this situation the ATO will notify your superannuation fund and the fund will need to assess whether your contribution could have been made as a personal contribution. If it could be accepted as a personal contribution, it will count towards the relevant contributions cap. If it cannot be accepted, then your super fund will need to return your contribution.

? FAQ

If I sell my home of 30 years four months before my 65th birthday, can I request an extension from the ATO to make my downsizer contribution until after I turn 65?

You can by all means ask the ATO but the reality is that the ATO would deny such a request merely to allow you to meet the age requirement. I would suggest deferring the settlement to such time that it's within 90 days of your 65th birthday.

63 COMPULSORY EMPLOYER CONTRIBUTIONS

When you are employed, your employer must pay super (known as superannuation guarantee (SG) contributions) on your behalf into a complying super fund. The introduction of the compulsory SG in 1992 has seen a huge boost in superannuation balances for Australians over the past two decades.

SG contributions are paid every quarter by your employer at a minimum of 9.50 per cent of your ordinary time earnings, up to the maximum contribution base. The payments count towards your concessional contributions cap. You may be able to choose the fund that this super is paid into, provided it is a complying super fund.

👍 TAX FACT

The government has strengthened the tax laws to counter fraudulent phoenix activity (where companies intentionally accumulate debts to improve cash flow or wealth and then liquidate to avoid paying the debt). The law changes are designed to protect workers' entitlements and strengthen directors' obligations by:

- extending the director penalty regime and the estimates regime to include the unpaid superannuation guarantee charge
- ensuring that directors cannot discharge their director penalties by placing their company into administration or liquidation when any pay as you go (PAYG) withholding or superannuation guarantee charge remains unpaid and unreported three months after the date that it is due for payment
- making directors and their associates liable to PAYG withholding non-compliance tax.

From 1 July 2021, the SG will increase by 0.5 per cent rises each financial year until the SG reaches 12 per cent in 2025–26.

You are only entitled to have SG contributions paid on your behalf from your boss if you are aged 18 years and over and you are paid $450 or more before tax in a month. It doesn't matter whether your employment status is full time or casual or if you're only a temporary resident of Australia.

Contractors who are paid wholly or principally for their labour are considered employees for SG purposes and must have 9.50 per cent SG contributions paid on their behalf under the same scenario as employees.

Ordinary time earnings are used to work out any SG contributions payable for employees. They are usually what you earn during ordinary hours of work and include allowances, bonuses, commissions and any over-award payments. Ordinary time earnings exclude annual leave loadings, expense reimbursements and any overtime payments.

👆 TAX FACT

The maximum contribution base limits the maximum amount of super support that employers have to provide each quarter. It's indexed annually. For the 2019–20 year the limit is $55 270 per quarter (equivalent to an annual salary of $221 080). Your employer doesn't have to pay SG contributions for any earnings above this limit. The 2018–19 federal budget proposed that the government will allow individuals who have multiple employers (and whose income exceeds $263 157) to nominate that their wages from certain employers are not subject to the superannuation guarantee to avoid inadvertently breaching the annual $25 000 concessional cap.

💡 TIP

If you are worried that your employer isn't paying the correct amount of super into your fund, the first thing to do is to double check with them. If your query isn't resolved you can contact the ATO, which will follow up further with an investigation into your employer's affairs.

Superannuation contributions made from personal injury payments are excluded from counting towards your non-concessional contributions cap for a financial year.

Employers must include the date that they intend to pay accrued superannuation on payslips provided to employees. Employers must also advise of the date that they last paid contributions on behalf of employees.

64 SALARY SACRIFICE

Perhaps the most tax-effective way to contribute money into super is via salary-sacrifice contributions, where you enter into an agreement with your employer to have some of your salary paid into your super fund instead of being paid to you. This has significant tax advantages if you earn over $18 200 (where the marginal tax rate jumps from zero to 21 per cent) as the contribution into super is only taxed at 15 per cent. Salary-sacrifice contributions count towards the concessional contributions cap.

Salary sacrificing into superannuation is one of the best legitimate ways of minimising your income tax bill.

The benefits of salary sacrificing include:

* super contributions are deductible for your employer
* your assessable income is reduced and potentially subject to a lower marginal rate
* money put into super is only taxed at 15 per cent instead of your marginal tax rate (potentially 47 per cent).

- The concessional tax rate of 15 per cent is capped at $25 000 into super each year. The rate increases to 30 per cent for individuals with income greater than $250 000.
- Any salary-sacrificed amounts will be reportable employer superannuation contributions that are included on your payment summary and will affect the income tests for the Medicare levy surcharge and some tax offsets and government benefits.
- Money can be tied up in super and you have to wait until retirement to access it.
- Payment of the sacrificed amounts above the compulsory SG is not required by regulation to be made quarterly, as is the SG.
- Some employers neglect to pay employees' super, particularly if they are close to bankruptcy and are having cash-flow difficulties.

> **⚠ PITFALL**
>
> Salary sacrifice is a relatively straightforward strategy, but it's crucial that you crunch the numbers correctly because any contributions made that exceed the respective cap will be taxed at 47 per cent rather than the 15 per cent (or 30 per cent) concessional tax rate.

65 DIVISION 293 TAX

Over the years there has been a great incentive for those taxpayers on the top marginal tax rate of 47 per cent to whack in as much money as possible into super and be taxed at the more generous concessional tax rate of 15 per cent and essentially locking in a 32 per cent tax saving on any contributions. This benefit was recently reduced but not totally diminished with the introduction of Division 293 into the Tax Act.

Division 293 tax is an additional tax on super contributions which reduces the tax concession for individuals whose combined adjusted taxable income and contributions are greater than the Division 293 threshold of $250 000. Division 293 tax is charged at an additional 15 per cent (effectively 30 per cent in total) of an individual's taxable contributions during the financial year that they exceeded the $250 000 threshold. There is no Division 293 tax to pay if you did not have any taxable contributions in the year.

⚠ PITFALL

Even though your income may not normally be in excess of $250 000, certain events can increase it to beyond this level for a particular year including eligible termination payments and capital gains. In these situations you will be liable for the extra 15 per cent Division 293 tax on your contributions into super for that year.

♦ TAX FACT

Division 293 tax is only levied on your concessional contributions for the year. There is no tax on non-concessional contributions and any earnings are subject to the standard 15 per cent concessional tax rate.

If you are over the income threshold, the ATO will issue a Division 293 notice generally several months after the end of the financial year once they match your tax return with information sent to them by your super fund on contributions made. You can elect to have monies released from your super fund to pay the amount outstanding rather than using your own funds.

If the extra tax payable relates to a defined benefit interest then the debt is deferred until a super benefit is paid with interest accruing based on the average 10-year Treasury bond rate (currently 2.7021 per cent).

♀ TIP

If you expect to have a Division 293 tax payable and you operate a self-managed superannuation fund, consider an investment strategy which generates fully franked dividends with imputation credits at 30 per cent to partially or wholly negate the impact of the additional tax.

66 SUPER CO-CONTRIBUTION

The term 'super co-contribution' should really be labelled as 'free money'! But it is surprising how few people actually take advantage of this great benefit.

Super co-contribution has been a government initiative since 2005 to help grow the superannuation balances for low and middle income earners. If you earn less than $53 564, you can take advantage of the super co-contribution payment by making a maximum personal super contribution of $1000 into your super fund. The government will then match it by 50 per cent up to a further $500.

If you qualify for the co-contribution, you do not need to do anything other than make the actual personal super contributions to your super fund and lodge your income tax return. There is no separate form or application to complete. The personal super contribution must be paid into a complying super fund and must not have been claimed as an income tax deduction. You can contact your super fund to find out how to make such a contribution.

The ATO outlines the two income tests you must satisfy to be eligible for the super co-contribution:

- the income threshold test
- the 10 per cent eligible income test.

The income threshold test

According to the ATO, if your total income (assessable income plus reportable fringe benefits total plus reportable employer super contributions less allowable deductions) is under the lower income threshold of $38 564 and you contribute $1000 post-tax into your super fund, the government will match it with a further $500. The super co-contribution gradually phases out to nil (by 3.333 cents per dollar) at the higher income threshold of $53 564.

> ✎ **EXAMPLE**
>
> Luke is an employee whose assessable income, reportable fringe benefits and reportable super contributions total $39 000. During the 2019–20 year he contributes $3000 as a personal super contribution to his super fund.
>
> Luke will receive $485 from the government as a co-contribution calculated as follows:
>
> $$\$500 - [(\$39\,000 - \$38\,564) \times \$0.03333]$$

Pierre is 71 and transfers his super interest of $248 000 from France to Australia. He satisfied the work test and over his lifetime he has made non-concessional contributions of $320 000 to Australian funds. As he is over 65 he cannot contribute more than the first $100 000 taking him to the annual non-concessional contribution limit, he must return the excess $148 000 to his French super fund. In subsquent years he could contribute more provided he continues to satisfy the work test.

You also need to pay income tax on the 'applicable fund earnings' component of a foreign fund transfer. These are the earnings on your foreign super balance that have accrued only since you became an Australian resident. None of your foreign super is treated as applicable fund earnings if you transfer it to Australia within six months of becoming an Australian resident.

💡 **TIP**

According to the ATO, if you elect to include some of your applicable fund earnings in your super fund's assessable income, rather than your own, your fund will pay the tax on the amount at 15 per cent, which could be less than the marginal rate of tax that you have to pay.

✎ **EXAMPLE**

Ryan emigrated to Australia in September 2010 when his foreign super balance was the equivalent of A$250 000. In May 2019, he transferred the balance to his Australian super fund when it was valued at A$350 000.

If Ryan makes no election, he must declare the $100 000 of 'applicable fund earnings' in his personal assessable income for the year which is taxed at his marginal tax rates. If he elects to include the applicable fund earnings into his super fund's assessable income, it is taxed at 15 per cent within the fund.

68 SELF MANAGED SUPERANNUATION FUNDS

As the name implies, a self managed super fund (SMSF) is a type of super fund that the members manage for their own benefit. SMSFs are growing in popularity as members' balances rise and they become more knowledgeable about managing their retirement savings. Over 25 000 new SMSFs were established in 2017–18 alone. The attractiveness of the concessional tax rules for super funds means that similar growth is expected to continue for some time yet.

👆 **TAX FACT**

The annual SMSF levy paid to the ATO is $259, payable in advance.

👆 **TAX FACT**

According to the ATO, there are now over 1127 300 members within 597 000 SMSFs in Australia holding just over $726 billion in retirement assets.

If you have the time as well as the expertise, including advisers you can call on, to devote to managing your investments, setting up an SMSF may be an option for you to look at for your retirement future.

💡 **TIP**

When considering the minimum balance to establish your own SMSF, you need to consider not only the amount and number of members, but also your risk profile because administration fees do vary among different investment strategies and they can eat up the benefits of doing it yourself. Results from my thesis indicate that, assuming the average expense ratio of 1.18 per cent for industry and retail funds, SMSFs are cost-effective for all balances when implementing a 100 per cent cash investment strategy, but are only cost-effective from $225 000 for sole members with a conservative profile, increasing to $325 000 for Balanced, $375 000 for Growth and $775 000 for High Growth (Raftery 2014).

Benefits of having an SMSF include:

- freedom to decide how and where to invest your superannuation funds
- tax benefits:
  - the maximum tax payable on contributions is 30 per cent and only 15 per cent for earnings in a complying SMSF. Capital gains tax on assets held more than 12 months is just 10 per cent.
  - earnings (including any capital gains) in the pension phase are not taxable (subject to the fund balance being under $1.6 million as at 1 July 2017 or subsequent date that the transfer balance account is created)
- economies of scale—when family members (up to four—proposed to increase to six from 1 July 2019) combine their superannuation funds the whole can become greater than the sum of its parts
- ability to invest in direct share portfolios—resulting imputation credits on dividends can help reduce the overall tax to be paid by the fund
- ability to invest in business real property
- deductible life insurance premiums
- rollover benefits—on retirement, assets can be rolled over into the pension phase and any capital gains subsequently realised will have no tax payable, provided that the fund balance is under $1.6 million on 1 July 2017 (or subsequent date that the transfer balance account is created). Amounts above this threshold will remain in accumulation phase and be subject to the normal 15 per cent tax on earnings in a complying SMSF.

While SMSFs can be great, they are not ideal for everyone. Before you establish one you should think carefully about some of the following issues:

- *Administrative obligations.* These may be onerous and include:
  - arranging an annual audit of your fund (proposed to be extended to a 3-yearly audit cycle for funds with a history of good record-keeping and compliance from 1 July 2019)

- keeping appropriate records
- reporting to the ATO on the fund's operation.

- *Annual charges.* Fees for administration, accounting, tax and audit can be expensive and range between $2000 and $6000 for an average-sized fund.

- *Compliance.* You need to be aware of the requirements of being an SMSF trustee as you are responsible for ensuring the fund complies with its trust deed and superannuation laws.

- *Management.* You need to manage the fund's investments in the best interests of fund members including ensuring they are for the sole purpose of providing retirement benefits and keeping them separate from the personal and business affairs of fund members.

⚠ PITFALL

If a SMSF loses its complying status because it didn't follow the laws and rules, it may incur the financial penalty of being taxed at 45 per cent instead of the concessional tax rate.

? FAQ

I'm thinking about setting up a SMSF. If I do, can I use my super monies to trade?

I would be extremely cautious about trading via a SMSF because super funds are technically not allowed to operate a business. I would encourage any share activities to be done as an investor rather than as a trader. You can purchase (and sell) exchange traded options as part of a hedging strategy but any premiums paid (or received) will need to be shown as CGT events. Remember that any investing must be in accordance with your written investment strategy for the fund in order to comply with the *SIS Act*. Be particularly careful with any investment in CFDs as funds deposited as security for obligations to pay margins will contravene the *SIS Act* as this is effectively a charge over fund assets.

? FAQ

Can my super fund purchase an apartment 'off the plan'?

It is possible but you will need to be careful because there can be some issues along the way. The deposit, stamp duty and any other costs to secure the purchase upfront must be paid using existing cash funds in super. Only when the unit is completed and strata titled can finance be used to complete the purchase. Seeking professional advice is recommended.

71 ACCESSING YOUR SUPER

Provided your super fund's deed allows it, you can access your super:

- when you retire after reaching your preservation age
- when you turn 65
- under the transition to retirement rules, while continuing to work.

Your preservation age, different from your pension age, is the age you must reach before you can access your super and depends on when you were born. The preservation age, currently 57, is gradually increasing to age 60 by 1 July 2024.

♀ TIP

If you are a temporary resident who worked and earned super while visiting Australia, you can apply to have your super paid to you as a departing Australia superannuation payment (DASP) after you have left our shores and your visa has expired or been cancelled. An application can be made via the DASP online application system with proof of identity required for superannuation fund balances over $5000. Although there are no application fees, the ATO will deduct tax as follows:

- 0 per cent for any tax-free component
- 38 per cent for a taxed element of a taxable component
- 47 per cent for an untaxed element of a taxable component
- 65 per cent for either taxed or untaxed elements of a taxable component if the temporary resident is a working holiday maker (that is, a backpacker).

Whether or not the ATO taxes your withdrawal of super funds will depend on your age and whether your super fund is a taxed or untaxed fund.

Most people have their super monies in a taxed super fund, where tax has already been paid on contributions going in and on earnings derived. If you are 60 years or older, any funds that you withdraw from your super fund will be tax-free if the fund is a taxed source. If you're under 60 the taxable component is treated as assessable income.

Regardless of your age, any income from an untaxed fund needs to be shown as assessable income in your tax return and is taxed at your marginal rate.

74 DEATH BENEFITS

Since superannuation became compulsory 27 years ago, retirement nest eggs have grown substantially and are an integral part of most estate planning. Premature death may mean a large payment to family members, particularly when a life insurance policy is attached to the fund.

♀ TIP

Superannuation does not form part of your estate. If you don't put a 'binding nomination' in place, the trustee of your super fund has absolute discretion in distributing your super benefits to anyone they please.

To ensure that your super funds are properly dealt with upon your death, make a 'binding nomination' with the super fund trustee. Binding nominations must be witnessed by two independent individuals and expire every three years, so make sure that you always update them.

👍 TAX FACT

Unlike other countries, there is no inheritance tax in Australia. But don't be fooled because there are three things in life that are certain: taxes, death ... and taxes on death!

If a death benefit is going to a dependant, such as a spouse or minor children, then it can be paid either as an income stream or as a lump-sum amount. Lump-sum payments to dependants are tax-free. However, a death benefit can only be paid as a lump sum to a non-dependant.

The popularity of superannuation as a low-tax environment within which to grow wealth, coupled with longer life expectancies, has resulted in an increasing number of financially independent people receiving a superannuation death benefit from a parent.

⚠ PITFALL

Lump-sum payments to non-dependants are taxed at 17 per cent on the taxed element while the untaxed element is taxed at a maximum rate of 32 per cent.

If you don't have a dependant to pay your death benefit to, there are a few strategies that you can use that can make a big difference to the final amount of tax payable. Accordingly, it is recommended that you discuss succession issues with a professional adviser.

If you are suffering from a terminal illness, you may want to consider withdrawing your entire super as a lump sum tax-free so that upon death it passes through your will to your independent family members tax-free as well.

Alternatively, consider withdrawing your super and then making non-concessional super contributions up to the non-concessional three-year bring forward limit so that any superannuation death benefit will comprise a tax-free element.

> **♀ TIP**
>
> A child-allocated pension is a smart way for a child to inherit their parent's super together with any linked life insurance. To make sure that a child pension can be activated when it's needed, the super fund needs to have the child listed as a beneficiary of their parent's account.

75 LOST OR UNCLAIMED SUPER

We work hard for our money, so it is surprising that so many people ignore one of their biggest assets: super. You should always keep track of your super by checking your annual statements for employer contributions, fees and insurance cover, and you should analyse fund performance in general.

> **♀ TIP**
>
> You may have worked in 12 different jobs but that is no excuse to have a dozen super funds. They are too hard to manage and may be eaten up in fees. Consolidate them by rolling them all into one fund. Make sure you arrange adequate replacement life insurance if you had coverage in existing accounts before closing them down.

Part VII is designed to help you stay in control of your tax affairs during the various stages of your business. Tax is the biggest expense that a business will encounter. As your business grows and changes, so will your tax situation. There will be additional tax obligations such as how to pay employees and other businesses and how to report and pay tax and superannuation.

76 CHOOSING THE RIGHT BUSINESS STRUCTURE

If you are planning to make a fortune, perhaps you should consider your business structure before you give away half of it in taxes.

> **♀ TIP**
>
> According to the ATO, the particular structure chosen needs to be appropriate to the business owner's specific circumstances and take into account likely events in the future (such as getting married, having children or admitting new partners).

The structure of a business will affect:

- how much tax your business has to pay
- how other businesses deal with you
- your administration costs
- your level of asset protection.

> **♀ TIP**
>
> Small businesses need all the help they can get but simply can't afford it on a full-time basis. Don't view external advice purely as a cost exercise. Sometimes you need to pay a bit extra to surround yourself with a group of quality advisers such as an accountant and a solicitor to help get the business on the right track for financial success.

The most common structures used by Australian businesses are:

- sole traders
- partnerships
- companies
- trusts.

Activity statements

Businesses are required to complete an activity statement to report and pay a number of tax obligations, such as GST, PAYG instalments, PAYG withholding and fringe benefits tax (FBT).

All businesses registered for GST need to regularly lodge a BAS with the ATO on either a monthly (21 days after period end), quarterly (28 October, 28 February, 28 April and 28 July) or annual basis (before lodgement due date for income tax return). Any GST paid on purchases is offset against the GST collected from customers. The net amount is remitted to the ATO via your BAS.

Large entities — those with a turnover of $20 million or more — are required to make PAYG income tax instalments monthly, rather than quarterly.

If you receive cryptocurrency for goods or services you provide as part of your business, you need to include the value of the cryptocurrency in Australian dollars as part of your ordinary income. This is the same process as receiving any other non-cash consideration under a barter transaction.

I'm about to get a car under my company and will be using it approximately 70 per cent for work and 30 per cent personal. In order to avoid FBT I will pay for my personal expenses incurred. Do I still need to register for FBT?

Yes you will still need to register for FBT and submit an FBT return each year, even if the net FBT payable is zero because you make a personal contribution.

If you want to manage your business tax affairs online with the ATO, there is a Business Portal available on the ATO website. It is safe to use as your information is protected by online security credentials. You must get a digital certificate from the ATO in order to use it on your computer. You can view your statement of account, update contact details, and prepare and lodge activity statements.

In 2015–16, the ATO conducted almost 1000 audits into phoenix schemes and raised liabilities of around $250 million. Over the three years to 30 June 2018, the ATO will spend $26.5 million on GST compliance activities alone.

78 RECORD KEEPING

While it is a legal requirement that you keep business records for tax purposes, it is also a good idea to keep excellent records in order to maximise your income tax return claims.

80 TRADING STOCK

The ATO defines trading stock as anything you produce, manufacture, acquire or purchase for manufacture, sale or exchange in your business, including livestock.

If the value of your trading stock at the end of the income year is:

- more than at the start of the financial year—the difference is added to your assessable income
- less than at the start of the financial year—a deduction can be claimed for the difference.

Small businesses only need to make an adjustment to their taxable income if their closing stock varies by more than $5000 from their opening stock figure.

👆 TAX FACT

If the value of the trading stock of a small business varies by less than $5000, you can elect to treat the value of closing stock as the same as opening stock at the start of the year for tax purposes.

An annual stocktake is usually conducted by businesses, generally as close as possible to the end of the financial year, to determine the value of trading stock on hand at 30 June.

⚠ PITFALL

If you run a business that sells food and you take an item for private use, such as milk or a meal, you must account for it as if you had sold it and include the value of the item in your assessable income. Owners can either keep a tab of the actual value of items used for private purposes or apply a standard amount from the ATO for your industry.

Taxation Determination TD 2019/2 provides the amount that the ATO will accept as estimates for the value of goods taken from trading stock for private use by taxpayers in different industries. Amounts range from $800 per adult per annum for a fruiterer business to $4640 per adult per annum for a licensed restaurant/cafe.

Irrespective of how they are valued for accounting purposes, there are only three methods allowed for valuing your trading stock for tax purposes:

- cost
- market selling value
- replacement value.

💡 TIP

The best stock valuation method to adopt is the method that produces the lowest value of trading stock. If you have different classes of stock then you can use a different basis of valuation for each class as well as for each individual item of stock, although these calculations can get messy.

You can change the method used each year so long as the opening stock figure is the same as the closing stock figure from the previous year.

💡 TIP

If you have some old plant or stock that your business simply can't sell, consider physically writing it off before 30 June and get a tax deduction for it this year.

You may be able to claim the business-related portion of the following 'running' costs:

- depreciation of home-office furniture, fittings and equipment such as computers and desks (certain items under $30000—reducing to $1000 after 1 July 2020—can be claimed in full by small businesses that choose the simpler depreciation rules—see tip 85 for more information).
- heating, cooling and lighting
- home telephone
- internet access
- printer and printer cartridges
- repairs to your home-office furniture and fittings
- stationery.

⚠ PITFALL

If you run your business from your own home, there is a possibility that your home could be subject to capital gains tax. Make sure you consult a tax adviser about your own particular circumstances. Sometimes it may be cheaper to pay for separate office space rather than incur a big tax bill in the future.

The ATO is quite particular with the claiming of home-office 'occupancy' expenses. If you genuinely operate a business from your home you are allowed to claim a proportion of mortgage interest or rent based on the actual floor space that you use for the business.

🖢 TAX FACT

If your home is your place of business, you can also claim a deduction for your occupancy expenses including:

- council rates
- home-insurance premiums
- mortgage interest
- rent.

The ATO looks at a number of factors to determine if your home is your place of business. The area must be:

- clearly identifiable as a place of business
- not readily suitable for use for private purposes
- used almost exclusively for business purposes
- used regularly for visits by clients or customers.

Home office deductions are usually calculated as follows:

Floor area used × relevant expenditure ÷ total floor area

✏ EXAMPLE

If your home office is 6 m x 3 m (that is, 18 square metres) and the total house is 100 square metres in size, you can claim 18 per cent of your occupancy costs for income tax purposes.

⚠ PITFALL

The ATO considers that any initial website development costs are capital in nature and only deductible over five years. However, website running costs (such as the annual domain name registration, site hosting, ongoing content and technical maintenance) are deemed to be operating costs that are claimable in the year that they are incurred.

♀ TIP

If the ATO conducts an audit into your business affairs, it will not accept estimates, so you must be quite accurate with your calculations. I recommend getting your measuring tape out and writing down the dimensions of your office and your overall house. I find it also helps to strengthen your case if you take photos of your office, especially if you move house down the track.

83 SHARING ECONOMY

The last five years have seen a surge of the sharing economy with Uber, GoCatch, Airbnb, Stayz, Spacer and Airtasker just to name a few who have become household names, not just in Australia but right across the globe.

> **👍 TAX FACT**
>
> During the 2016–17 and 2017–18 financial years, the ATO matched data for up to 60 000 individuals who provided ride-sourcing services (such as Uber).

Not only are we becoming trusted users of these services, more and more people (if my mates are any guides) are themselves offering these services and picking up a bit of extra money for the household each week on top of their normal salary. What is really important is that if you provide goods or services through any of these apps or websites, you have tax obligations with all payments you receive through the sharing economy being subject to income tax after allowing for deductions for associated expenses.

You will be considered to be operating a business which will require an ABN and you must declare the income in the business income section in your tax return.

> **👍 TAX FACT**
>
> Assessable income from the sharing economy may include:
> * income earned from performing services for a fee
> * ride-sourcing services for a fare (considered a taxi travel service for GST purposes)
> * food delivery
> * tasking or other odd jobs arranged through a sharing economy platform
> * renting out a room or a whole property that you own or lease (such as your home, a rental property or a parking space) for a short-time basis
> * income from sharing other forms of property, such as a motor vehicle or caravan.

If your turnover is over $75 000 per year, you may be required to register for GST and lodge quarterly business activity statements. While there is no GST on residential rent, all ride-sourcing enterprises must have an ABN and be registered for GST regardless of turnover.

⚠ PITFALL

If you rent out a parking space, you may need to pay CGT when you eventually sell it or property it's attached to. A small bit of income now may lead to large unexpected tax liability in the future.

You can claim income tax deductions relating to income you earn but if your expenses are for both business and private use, you can only claim a deduction for the business-related portion. Any fees or commissions charged by a sharing economy facilitator can be claimed as a deduction.

💡 TIP

If you are concerned you might get a tax bill because you think your business will generate a profit, you can choose to make a prepayment of tax rather than wait for the nasty tax bill at the end of the year. This voluntary payment made in advance can be made at any time and as often as you like to make it easier for you to manage your tax.

? FAQ

I am thinking about letting out a room for a night here and there to travellers via one of those online sites such as Airbnb. Would I need to declare the money received as income? What are the implications, if any, if I don't declare it?

The tax rules are pretty clear. Any rental income that you receive — no matter how small — needs to be declared as assessable income in your return and you'll need to pay tax on it.

Trying to dodge the tax office by not declaring the income will end in tears. You may think that the income is so little that the ATO won't bother, but the cash economy is huge and is definitely on the tax man's hit list. Something like this is advertised on the internet so the ATO is more likely to find out about it. Guests are paying electronically, which makes it easier to track down. I should also warn that people renting rooms in their home also need to be aware it's probably opening them up to capital gains tax when they sell their homes down the track.

84 EMPLOYING PEOPLE

So you took the first step and started your own business. Now business has gone crazy and sales are through the roof and you need to hire someone else to help you in handling the growth.

While it is always exciting when a small business starts to grow and you need to employ staff for the first time, you need to be aware of some of the obligations that come with being an employer. Non-compliance could lead to penalties, which include fines and prosecution.

Wages and conditions

All issues concerning wages and employment conditions in the private sector fall under the *Fair Work Act 2009*, which requires you to maintain a minimum standard of pay, conditions and entitlements for your employees. There are 10 National Employment Standards that apply to all employers and employees.

Employment records

You must issue pay slips to each employee and keep accurate and complete time and wages records for a minimum of seven years.

Taxation obligations

Your taxation obligations include:

- registering with the ATO as a new employer
- obtaining *TFN declarations* (NAT 3092) from employees
- withholding PAYG tax from payments you make to your employees and paying it to the ATO
- preparing year-end PAYG payment summaries for employees
- calculating any employment termination payments
- paying fringe benefits tax for benefits paid to employees
- paying payroll tax if total wages exceed the exemption threshold applicable in your state or territory:

- ACT: 6.85 per cent over $2 000 000
- NSW: 5.45 per cent over $900 000
- Northern Territory: 5.5 per cent over $1 500 000
- Queensland: 4.75 per cent over $1 100 000
- South Australia: 4.95 per cent over $1 500 000
- Tasmania: 4 per cent over $1 250 000
- Victoria: 4.85 per cent over $650 000
- Western Australia: 5.5 per cent over $850 000

♀ TIP

While they need to be provided by 14 July, your employees will appreciate it if you give them their annual PAYG payment summary as soon as possible after year end so they can complete their own tax returns.

👍 TAX FACT

From 1 July 2019 small employers with 19 or less employees will need to report tax and super information to the ATO through Single Touch Payroll which is available through most payroll, accounting and business management software.

Superannuation obligations

Employing people, whether full time, part time or casual, will trigger the superannuation guarantee legislation which requires you to pay a minimum of 9.50 per cent of the earnings base (generally ordinary time earnings) into employees' choice of super fund, via *SuperStream*, within 28 days after the end of the quarter.

⚠ PITFALL

If you don't pay your super obligations in time, then you are charged an interest shortfall penalty of 10 per cent per annum plus an administration fee of $20 per employee per quarter.

Holiday and leave entitlements

You need to pay public holidays for all employees except for those who are only paid for hours worked such as contract workers and casual employees. Other paid leave should include annual, sick and long-service leave.

Other employment issues to consider include:

- anti-discrimination
- equal employment opportunity
- occupational health and safety legislation
- public liability insurance
- workers compensation.

💡 TIP

How do good, profitable businesses go bad? Mainly because their owners took all of the cash out of their business before realising that they had to pay the tax man for GST and PAYG withholding in the quarterly BAS or income tax at the end of the year. Super payable to employees is another forgotten liability. To avoid falling into the trap, open up a separate bank account and filter one-third of your income away to cover these outgoings.

If you pay your employees in cryptocurrency the tax treatment will vary dependent on whether there is a valid salary sacrifice agreement in place or not. Where an employee has a valid salary sacrifice arrangement to receive cryptocurrency as remuneration instead of Australian dollars, the payment of the cryptocurrency is a fringe benefit and the employer is required to pay FBT.

In the absence of a valid salary sacrifice agreement, the employee is considered to have derived their normal salary or wages and the employer will need to meet their pay as you go obligations on the Australian dollar value of the cryptocurrency it pays to the employee.

85 TAX CONCESSIONS AND OFFSETS

Small businesses have access to a range of concessions to help reduce their taxable income, designed to make tax administration easier. For example, they are entitled to immediate tax deductions for business expenses prepaid for 12 months in advance, such as interest.

Simplified depreciation rules

Businesses with an annual turnover under $50 million can immediately write off many depreciating assets that cost less than $30 000 exclusive of GST. For businesses that are registered for GST, the effective ticket-price threshold is $32 999 as you can claim the 10 per cent GST rebate in your quarterly business activity statement.

⚠ PITFALL

Vehicles purchased through a company or trust structure may be subject to fringe benefits tax.

Small businesses can consolidate other assets in a general small business pool at a rate of 30 per cent. This pool can be immediately deducted if the balance is less than $30 000 before 30 June 2020.

Restart wage subsidy

Employers can receive up to $10 000 (GST inclusive) in government assistance if they hire a full-time job seeker aged 50 or older under the Restart wage subsidy program. Eligible employers will receive the payment if the job seeker was previously unemployed for a period of 6 months and subsequently employed for a minimum average of 20 hours per week. Employers may also be able to receive a kickstart payment of up to 40 per cent of the total wage subsidy after four weeks of a job starting.

Youth bonus wage subsidy

Eligible employers can receive up to $10 000 (GST inclusive) via the youth bonus wage subsidy if they hire a job seeker between 15 and 24 for a minimum average of 20 hours per week over six months.

Other wage subsidies

Eligible employers can receive up to $6500 (GST inclusive) if they hire the following job seekers for a minimum average of 20 hours per week over six months:

- youth wage subsidy—job seekers who are between 25 and 29 years of age

- parents wage subsidy—a job seeker who is a principal carer parent

- long-term unemployed and Indigenous wage subsidy—a long-term unemployed job seeker who has been registered with employment services for 12 months, or an Indigenous Australian job seeker who has been registered with employment services for six months.

Income averaging

Primary producers and special professionals (such as authors, inventors, performing artists, production assocociates and sportspersons) may have their income averaged out over a number of years to smooth out any unexpected high increases in tax due to the abnormal levels of income that are derived in one financial year.

Export Market Development Grant

Small and medium-sized businesses with annual turnover under $50 million can receive government assistance via the Export Market Development Grants (EMDG) scheme on developing export markets. Administered by Austrade, the EMDG scheme reimburses up to 50% of eligible export promotion expenses above $5000 (to a maximum of $150 000) provided that the total expenses are at least $15 000.

Fuel tax credits

Businesses can claim a credit for the fuel tax (excise or customs duty) that's included in the price of fuel used in:

- machinery
- plant
- equipment
- heavy vehicles
- light vehicles travelling off public roads or on private roads.

The rates of credit for fuel acquired range from 15.8 cents per litre for liquid fuels used by heavy vehicles travelling on public roads up to 41.6 cents per litre for fuels used for other business uses.

Research and development tax incentive

If your business is involved in research and development (R&D) in Australia to create new or improved materials, devices, processes, products or services it may be eligible for an R&D tax incentive. The Department of Innovation, Industry, Science and Research defines R&D activity as systematic, investigative and experimental activity that:

- involves both innovation and high levels of technical risk
- is for the process of producing new knowledge or improvements.

The R&D tax incentive is a 43.5 per cent refundable tax offset (proposed to change to a premium of 13.5 per cent above the claimant's company tax rate) for companies with an annual turnover less than $20 million.

Other eligible companies with a higher turnover are eligible for a 38.5 per cent non-refundable tax offset. However, since 1 July 2014, large businesses with annual Australian R&D claims in excess of $100 million (proposed to increase to $150 million) are limited in receiving the R&D tax incentive to that amount, but will be eligible to claim the excess R&D expenditure as a general deduction. The ATO looks after this incentive jointly with AusIndustry. In order to be eligible you need to register each income year with the Industry Research and Development Board and meet the minimum R&D threshold expenditure of $20000. The 2018-19 federal budget proposed a $4 million annual cap on cash refunds for R&D claimants with aggregated annual turnover less than $20 million.

Skills and Training Incentive

The Skills and Training Incentive assists older Australians to update their skills and stay in the workforce. The Incentive is available to 31 December 2020 to fund reskilling opportunities for individuals aged 45 to 70 who are susceptible to job loss and have completed a Skills Checkpoint for Older Workers Program. The incentive is up to $2200 (including GST) per worker and is to be matched by either the individual or the employer.

86 SELLING OR CLOSING DOWN

If you close down or sell your business, there are significant opportunities to do some tax planning and minimise CGT as much as possible.

If you are a retiring small business owner you may be entitled to disregard some or all of your capital gains if you:

- are 55 years or over
- retired or are permanently incapacitated
- owned your 'small business CGT assets' for 15 years or more.

If you do not satisfy the above criteria, the ATO says you may still be entitled to the following concessions to reduce any potential taxable capital gain from the sale of your small business:

- 50 per cent general CGT discount—for capital gains on assets that you have held for 12 months or more
- small business 50 per cent active asset reduction—reduces the capital gains on 'active assets' by 50 per cent
- small business retirement exemption—disregards any remaining capital gain by up to a lifetime limit of $500 000 per individual if paid into a complying superannuation fund
- small business asset rollover—defers a capital gain where you acquire 'replacement assets'.

To qualify for these small business concessions, the ATO says you must satisfy the following conditions:

- You have been carrying on a business with a turnover under $2 million.
- The net value of your CGT assets and any related entities is a maximum of $6 million.
- Your CGT asset is an 'active asset'.

- If the asset is a share or interest in a trust:
  - there must be a 'controlling individual' just before the CGT event
  - the entity claiming the concession must be a 'CGT concession stakeholder' in the company.

When doing capital gains tax calculations on your home used for a business, the ATO allows you to have acquired it for its market value on the day when the property was first used to produce assessable income.

87 PERSONAL SERVICES INCOME

If you are a contractor or a consultant and you operate your business via a partnership, company or trust, you need to ensure that you satisfy the personal services income (PSI) rules, as you run the risk of being personally liable for tax on the income regardless of your business structure. The rules can also deny deductions for some business-related expenses incurred as a contractor.

If the majority of your income is for labour rather than for materials supplied or tools and equipment used to complete the job, then you will be subject to the PSI rules.

There is an exemption from the PSI rules if you pass the results test, which is a test to work out if you've received the income after achieving a specific result or outcome.

To pass the results test, you need to satisfy all three of the following conditions for at least three quarters of the year:

- you are paid income to achieve a specified result or outcome
- you provide tools and equipment as contracted in order to perform the work
- you are liable for rectifying any defects in the work.

If you fail the results test, you need to apply an additional rule, known as the 80/20 rule, under which you can't generate more than 80 per cent of your income from one client and you must also satisfy one of the following conditions:

- you have received income from two or more clients who are not connected or related (unrelated clients test)
- you employed or contracted others to help complete the work (employment test)
- you used a separate premises exclusively for business (business premises test).

You can also apply for a determination from the ATO for an exemption from the rules, but it is generally only allowed in exceptional circumstances.

> ### ⚠ PITFALL
>
> If you fail the results and 80/20 tests for the PSI rules then you must:
>
> - pay any retained profits from PSI as a salary and wage to the individual who performed the services
> - comply with the additional PAYG obligations
> - complete and attach a PSI schedule with your tax return
> - not claim deductions against PSI where there is no entitlement, such as council rates, interest or rent for your home office, or payments to your spouse for secretarial work.

88 NON-COMMERCIAL LOSSES

Losses are sometimes unavoidable in business, particularly in the start-up years. For individuals and partnerships, if you have a net loss from a business activity, the non-commercial loss rules apply. These rules determine whether you can use your business loss to offset income from other sources, such as salary and wages, interest and dividends.

> ### 👆 TAX FACT
>
> The non-commercial legislation was introduced to stop 'Pitt Street farmers' (the main street in the Sydney business district) from claiming huge losses on their farms, primarily used as holiday homes, against their normal salary and wage income.

Each year that a business makes a net loss, the owner must consider whether they can claim the loss in the current tax return or whether it's necessary to defer the loss until future profits are made.

The non-commercial losses rules limit the ability of taxpayers to offset business losses against other assessment income unless one or more of the following tests are met:

- assessable income generated by the business is at least $20 000 (assessable income test)
- the business shows a profit for at least three out of the past five years (profits test)
- the business has property or an interest in real property with a value of at least $500 000 on a continuing basis (real property test)
- the business has at least $100 000 of other assets being used on a continuing basis (other assets test).

89 FRANCHISING

If your business becomes quite successful you may toy with the thought of franchising it so that other people can pay you copious amounts of cash for your idea. Sounds really good in theory but you need excellent systems, patience and time to set it up properly.

Franchising is a highly complicated area with huge scope for franchisors to be sued by franchisees if you don't comply with the franchising laws correctly. It is strongly recommended that you hire expert franchising consultants to ensure that you get excellent advice in establishing the franchise correctly.

♀ TIP

Ensure that you have a new company to hold the intellectual property (IP) and another separate company from your original trading company to house the head franchisor. This structure will help protect your assets should the unthinkable occur.

According to the ATO, payments received from the franchisee—such as advertising costs, the initial franchise fee, service fees, royalties and training fees—will form part of the franchisor's assessable income for income tax purposes. As these payments are likely to be over $75 000 per annum the franchisor will need to register for GST and charge it accordingly. The franchisor will need to report and remit the GST to the ATO on a quarterly basis. If the franchisee is GST registered, they can claim a GST credit in their business activity statement for the GST paid to the franchisor.

⚠ PITFALL

It can be very costly (as much as $250 000) to set up the correct franchising structure as well as complying with all of the requirements of the Franchising Code of Conduct administered through the Australian Competition and Consumer Commission (ACCC).

You also need to maintain a separate set of financial records for each company created in the structure, resulting in higher administration fees such as accounting, tax, audit and Australian Securities and Investments Commission annual return fees.

PART VIII

MISCELLANEOUS

Wouldn't it be great if the tax system fitted nicely into seven parts? Unfortunately, tax legislation is wide and varied. And it will only continue to grow in years to come as the only constant with tax is change.

Part VIII looks at a few more concessions that are available to taxpayers as well as some of the administrative aspects of taxation such as lodgements, penalties, data matching and what to do if you have problems paying your tax debt. I'll also look at earning income overseas and tell you how to get a great accountant.

▲ PITFALL

While income-protection insurance is deductible, individuals cannot claim a tax deduction for life insurance. Life insurance is only deductible within super.

90 OVERSEAS INCOME

The tax treatment of foreign income by Australian tax residents can be complicated, particularly when foreign tax credits are added into the equation.

✎ TAX FACT

If you are an Australian resident, you are taxed on worldwide income. Any foreign income will need to be included in your tax return as assessable income and you may be entitled to a foreign income tax offset for amounts of foreign tax paid. Non-residents are only taxed on their Australian-sourced income.

The ATO considers you an Australian resident for tax purposes if you meet any of the following conditions:

- you are born and bred in Australia
- you are living permanently in Australia
- you have been living in Australia for at least six months and working the majority of that time at the same job and living at the same place

⚠ PITFALL

Pensioners who live or travel overseas for more than six weeks will have their pension paid at the 'outside Australia' rate. After 26 weeks of overseas travel, the pension rate is revised and based on how long you lived in Australia between the age of 16 and the age pension age. Since 1 January 2017 pensioners who have lived in Australia for fewer than 35 years will be paid a reduced pension proportional to their Australian working life residence ratio.

- you have been living in Australia for more than half of the financial year, except where your usual home is overseas and you do not intend to live in Australia permanently.

If you are an Australian resident who is engaged in foreign service for a continuous period of 91 days or more you may be eligible for an exemption on Australian tax on this employment income if your employer:

- provides Australian official development assistance
- operates and maintains a public fund for disaster relief for people in a developing country
- is exempt from Australian income tax
- is an Australian Government authority that has deployed you outside Australia as a member of a disciplined force.

⚠ PITFALL

If you have a foreign currency denominated bank account with a balance greater than A$250 000, you may be subject to Australian tax on any realised foreign currency gains or losses, even if you are merely depositing money and making withdrawals.

If you think you don't need to declare your overseas income then think again. The ATO has tax treaties with 45 countries that allow them to exchange information about offshore income and transactions. Any data received is matched against Australian tax returns.

The ATO also receives information from the Australian Transaction Reports and Analysis Centre (AUSTRAC), which monitors domestic and international transactions over $10 000.

If you have been an Australian resident but you leave Australia, then you need to be aware that:

- you are still taxed in Australia on any Australian-sourced income
- any overseas assets are deemed to be disposed for capital gains tax purposes, potentially giving rise to a tax liability
- any HELP or SFSS debts will continue to be indexed.

👍 **TAX FACT**

Since the 2016–17 income year, graduates living overseas and earning incomes above the minimum HELP repayment threshold (see p. 71) will be required to make repayments towards their HELP debts based on their worldwide income.

💡 **TIP**

If you move overseas and become a non-resident, notify your bank (regarding interest) and share registries (dividends), so that withholding tax is deducted at the source and you will have no further tax obligation in Australia for this income, including not needing to disclose it in your Australian tax return.

💡 **TIP**

If you have worked overseas and had retirement benefits paid on your behalf then consider transferring the balance of your foreign pension account to your complying Australian superannuation fund. (For more information, see p. 169.)

91 GETTING A GREAT ACCOUNTANT

A friend once told me that there are two things in life that people need—a good mechanic and a great accountant.

Taxation is a complex area and deserves the attention of a specialist to give you the right advice to ensure you are maximising deductions yet staying within the regulations.

For some people, tax is a pain and they pay a small fee to get rid of the discomfort. But remember that if you pay peanuts, you get monkeys, so do not base your decision solely on price because a bad accountant could cost you thousands down the track due to a dodgy claim or missing a key strategy to save tax.

The most important thing is to pick an accountant who is a registered tax agent and also a member of a professional body. This at least provides you with some confidence that they are educated and keep reasonably up to date each year with the changing tax laws.

There are three professionally recognised accountancy bodies in Australia:

- Institute of Chartered Accountants in Australia and New Zealand (CAANZ) www.charteredaccountants.com.au
- CPA Australia www.cpaaustralia.com.au
- Institute of Public Accountants (IPA) www.publicaccountants.org.au

While it is nice to have an accountant who communicates well, it is more important that they are communicating the right information to you. Ask your friends for recommendations as they can report on their own experience. I also find that a well-constructed website with regular client newsletters and updates that are in plain, simple English is really important. Like mechanics, don't pick someone who treats you like a typical 'dumb' client but rather someone who takes the time to explain things in more depth.

👆 TAX FACT

According to the ATO, the average cost of managing tax affairs claimed by an individual in the 2016–17 financial year was $374.

💡 TIP

A great accountant, like a top doctor, is likely to be busy so don't get frustrated if they cannot see you at the drop of a hat.

People who don't send in their tax return by the due date may be charged late-lodgement penalties or may even be prosecuted. Penalties for late lodgement of tax returns can be as high as $1050, as well as good behaviour bonds and jail sentences. Since 1 July 2017, the late lodgement of business activity statements (BAS) incurs a fine of $210 for each month late, up to a maximum penalty of $1050 per BAS.

93 AMENDING RETURNS AND OBJECTING TO ASSESSMENTS

Amendments

Whether it is missed interest income or a deduction that you forgot to claim, it is possible to lodge a request with the ATO to amend your income tax return, even long after your original return was lodged and assessed. Generally the ATO has the power to amend returns for up to four years after lodgement of the original return.

> **🎁 BONUS RESOURCES**
>
> If you need to amend your tax return you can download and complete the ATO form *Request for amendment of income tax return for individuals* (NAT 2843) from the ATO website.

If you have made a mistake or need to amend your tax return, it is important you do so promptly. You can either download the ATO amendment request form or send a letter to the ATO (PO Box 3004, Penrith NSW 2740).

> **💡 TIP**
>
> If you wish to amend your tax return, ensure your amendment request letter contains the following information:
>
> - your name, address and contact phone number
> - your TFN
> - the income tax year that the amendment relates to
> - the reason for the amendment of the return
> - the item number of the tax return that requires amendment
> - the amount of the amendment
> - a declaration that all the information provided, including any attachments, is true and correct and that you have the necessary receipts and other records to support your claim for amendment.
>
> You will also need to sign and date the letter.

Objections

If the ATO issues you with a notice of assessment that you disagree with, you don't have to simply 'like it or lump it'. You generally have up to two years to submit an objection to your assessment with the ATO. If you are objecting to an ATO ruling, other than an assessment, then you generally have only 60 days to lodge your objection to their decision.

All objections must be in writing and signed and dated. You can either download the ATO objection form or send a letter to the ATO (PO Box 3524, Albury NSW 2640). The ATO will generally take eight weeks to make a decision about your objection. If you disagree with that decision then you can apply for an independent external review.

Ensure that your objection letter includes the following:

- your name, address and contact phone number
- your TFN
- the income tax year that the amendment relates to
- the reasons why you think that the ATO's original decision is wrong
- the relevant facts, arguments, information and documents that support the reasons you disagree with the ATO decision (including legislation, case law and rulings)
- a declaration that all the information provided, including any attachments, is true and correct
- any supporting documents and information that relate to the decision being reviewed.

Since 1 July 2014, the ATO has issued most individual taxpayers with a tax receipt in conjunction with the original notice of assessment as part of the annual income tax return process.

The tax receipt contains a table showing how your taxes have been allocated to key categories of government expenditure. It also includes information on the level of Australian Government gross debt for the current and previous years.

BONUS RESOURCES

If you want to lodge an objection you can download and complete the ATO form *Objection form—for taxpayers* (NAT 13471) from the ATO website.

TIP

You cannot formally object to the following:

- a general interest charge (GIC)
- a shortfall interest charge
- a late lodgement penalty.

However, you can still talk to the ATO if you disagree with their decision. The ATO will review your file and determine if those charges are still applicable.

94 ATO DATA MATCHING

Over the past five years, data matching has been a powerful tax compliance tool for the ATO. It has acted as a huge deterrent for taxpayers thinking about not disclosing all of their income.

TAX FACT

In 2014–15 the ATO recovered an extra $1.1 billion in adjustments after reviewing more than 650 million transactions and conducting over 450 000 data matching reviews.

95 PROBLEMS PAYING YOUR TAX

You must pay your tax as and when it falls due. But there are times when you simply cannot pay your tax and BAS obligations on time. If you are in this situation contact the ATO immediately to discuss your circumstances. ATO officers are very understanding of your situation and will be as fair and reasonable as possible with you.

> ♀ **TIP**
>
> Don't delay the lodgement of your outstanding tax and BAS returns simply because you don't have the money to pay, because there are penalties for late lodgement too.

It is likely that you will need to provide the ATO with your true financial position (such as a list of assets, liabilities, income and expenditure) to show that you are having difficulties meeting your debts as and when they fall due. Depending on your individual circumstances, you may be given an extension of time to pay the ATO.

> ⚠ **PITFALL**
>
> If you get an extension of time to pay your taxes, the ATO will impose a general interest charge (GIC), which accrues on your debt until it is paid off in full. The GIC, currently 8.96 per cent, is tax-deductible in the financial year in which it is charged.

Along with meeting your monthly repayments, you will need to ensure that any future tax returns and activity statements are lodged and paid on time. Failure to do so will be considered a default on your payment arrangement, and will require an explanation to the ATO.

Depending on your individual circumstances, the ATO has the ability to release you from some or all of your tax debts. If paying your tax would cause you 'serious hardship' by preventing you from providing the basic necessities (such as food, shelter, clothing and education) for yourself and your family, then you may apply for this concession.

Taxpayers in this situation will need to complete an 'application for release' form and provide supporting documentation showing how payment of the tax debt will cause serious hardship.

96 MEDICAL EXPENSES TAX OFFSET

It doesn't pay to get sick, particularly as doctors and medications are not cheap these days.

However, to help you with paying your costs you can claim, via your tax return, a rebate of 20 per cent of your net medical expenses (including those medical expenses of your dependants) for the amounts incurred over $2333 in a financial year.

The medical expenses tax offset covers 'the gap' that you pay after any refunds from Medicare or your private health fund. The expenses must be related to an illness or operation provided by a registered medical practitioner, including payments to doctors, nurses, dentists, orthodontists, opticians and optometrists. It also includes medical aids, medicines and therapeutic treatments prescribed by a doctor.

⚠ PITFALL

The net medical expenses tax offset has been phased out in recent years. Taxpayers can only claim the medical expenses tax offset in 2018–19 if they incurred out-of-pocket medical expenses relating to disability aids, attendant or aged care until 1 July 2019.

? FAQ

Can I claim the medical expenses tax offset for those expenses that have been funded by the NDIS?

Unfortunately you cannot include net medical expenses that have been funded by the NDIS. However, if you incur additional medical expenses that you pay for out of your own pocket then you may be eligible to claim this tax offset.

✏ EXAMPLE

Joe has incurred medical expenses in relation to disability aids and earns $50 000. He incurs medical expenses of $4000 for the 2017–18 financial year. He received $450 back from Medicare and a further $550 from his private health fund. In his tax return he can claim a rebate of $133, which is 20 per cent of his net medical expenses over $2333.

You can generally get an itemised annual statement from the following organisations to help you reconstruct your expenses:

- Medicare
- your private health fund

97 LEVIES

Medicare levy surcharge

For more than 35 years, the Medicare scheme has provided Australians with greater access to health care. It has been funded by a Medicare levy paid by individual taxpayers who are also Australian residents. The levy is charged by the ATO based on 2 per cent of your taxable income via your notice of assessment each year.

👍 TAX FACT

The Medicare levy was raised on 1 July 2014 by half a percentage point to 2 per cent to provide a funding stream for DisabilityCare Australia.

If you or your dependants do not have private health insurance and your 'adjusted taxable income' was above a certain amount, you may have to pay an additional Medicare levy surcharge on top of the standard 2 per cent levy.

⚠ PITFALL

If you are over 30 and don't have private health cover there are lifetime health cover penalties that apply when you subsequently take out cover. For each year over age 30 that you delay in getting basic hospital cover, you will have to pay an extra 2 per cent on your premium, up to a maximum of 70 per cent, when you finally take out the cover.

The Medicare levy surcharge is an additional levy of up to 1.5 per cent, charged on your adjusted taxable income, which is the sum of:

- your taxable income
- your reportable super contributions
- your net investment losses
- your total reportable fringe benefits
- any amount on which family trust distribution tax has been paid.

If you and your dependants have private health insurance, you may be eligible for a refundable tax rebate. It can be received as a refund even if you do not have to pay any tax. Similar to the Medicare levy surcharge, this private health rebate is affected by your income, marital status and age.

TABLE 8.1: Medicare levy surcharge and private health insurance rebate (singles) (2019–20)

Adjusted taxable income	Medicare levy surcharge	Rebate if under age 65	Rebate if aged 65–69 years	Rebate if over age 70
Up to $90 000	Nil	25.059%	29.236%	33.413%
$90 001–$105 000	1%	16.706%	20.883%	25.059%
$105 001–$140 000	1.25%	8.352%	12.529%	16.706%
over $140 000	1.5%	0%	0%	0%

Source: © Australian Taxation Office for the Commonwealth of Australia.

TABLE 8.2: Medicare levy surcharge and private health insurance rebate (couples or single parents) (2018–19)

Adjusted taxable income (total)*	Medicare levy surcharge	Rebate if under age 65	Rebate if aged 65–69 years	Rebate if over age 70
Up to $180 000	Nil	25.059%	29.236%	33.413%
$180 001–$210 000	1%	16.706%	20.883%	25.059%
$210 001–$280 000	1.25%	8.352%	12.529%	16.706%
Over $280 000	1.5%	0%	0%	0%

*The threshold rises by $1500 for each dependent child born after the first.
Source: © Australian Taxation Office for the Commonwealth of Australia.

If you know that you are going to fall above a higher income threshold (or you are unsure what your income level will be), then contact your private health provider at the start of the year and reduce the rebate that you receive upfront. Otherwise you might get a nasty surprise when you get your tax assessment and find out that you have to pay back a part or all of your rebate that you were not entitled to receive.

The income thresholds used to calculate the Medicare levy surcharge and private health insurance rebate will remain at the 2014–15 levels until 2020-21.

Those with incomes just below each threshold may move above a higher income threshold if their income increases (known as 'bracket creep'). For those with private health insurance, your rebate percentage entitlement may decrease. For those who do not have the appropriate level of private patient hospital cover, you may have to pay either the Medicare levy surcharge or if you paid the surcharge in the previous year, the rate of the surcharge may increase.

Consider prepaying up to 12 months of private medical cover before the end of the current tax year if you think your taxable income in the subsequent financial year will take you above one of the private health insurance rebate 'income thresholds' in table 8.1 (singles) and table 8.2 (couples). The situation might arise if you are planning on realising a large capital gain or perhaps receiving a big bonus after 30 June. By implementing this strategy you will be able to get the higher rebate percentage back to you in the current year.

98 ZONE AND OVERSEAS FORCES TAX OFFSETS

If you lived or worked in a remote area or served in forces overseas during the financial year you may be able to claim a tax offset.

Zone tax offset

This is often a forgotten claim—particularly if you use an accountant outside of the region where you live. The offset is available if you lived in a remote or isolated part of Australia, not including an offshore oil or gas rig, for at least half of the financial year.

📍 TAX FACT

The ATO classifies remote areas into two zones—zone A and zone B—and designates special areas within these zones. If you are unsure whether you are in a remote area, the ATO has an Australian zone list available on its website.

To qualify for the zone tax offset, you must have worked or lived in a remote area for 183 days or more during the current financial year or, if you haven't previously claimed the zone tax offset, 183 days or more in total during the current and previous financial years—but less than 183 days in the current year and less than 183 days in the previous financial year.

Note that the time spent in a remote area does not have to be continuous.

📍 TAX FACT

Since 1 July 2015, 'fly-in fly-out' and 'drive-in drive-out' workers are not eligible for the zone tax offset when their normal residence is not within a zone.

⚠ PITFALL

Some tax agents who live in capital cities do not automatically think of this tax offset, so it is wise to prompt them if you do live in a zone area.

Overseas forces tax offset

If you have served during the financial year in a specified overseas locality as a member of either the Australian defence forces or the United Nations forces, and your income relating to that service was not specifically exempt from tax, you may be eligible for an overseas forces tax offset.

To claim the full overseas forces tax offset, you must have served in one or more overseas localities for 183 days or more during the financial year. A portion of the offset may still be claimed even if your overseas service was fewer than 183 days.

The tax offset amounts are shown in table 8.3.

TABLE 8.3: zone and overseas forces tax offsets (2018–19)

Your circumstances	Zone A	Zone B	Special area	Overseas forces
You were single with no dependent child or student for whole of year	$338	$57	$1173	$338
You are able to claim the maximum dependant (invalid and carer) tax offset ($2717)	$1697	$600	$2532	$1697

Source: © Australian Taxation Office for the Commonwealth of Australia.

99 TAX-EFFECTIVE INVESTMENTS

Around May and June each year, there are a number of accountants and financial planners who try to promote tax-effective investments in agribusiness and forestry products.

The ATO has labelled these investments as 'aggressive tax planning' products and for good reason—these investments have copped a lot of bad press in recent years thanks to some projects going into administration, resulting in their investors losing potentially thousands of dollars.

Used the right way, they can be a very good tax-planning strategy; for example, they can help level out the tax on any capital gains or bonus during a financial year.

But sometimes these investments sound too good to be true. Potential investors must form their own view about the commercial and financial viability of the product. Take care before you invest because while you are getting a tax deduction you are still risking the amount not covered by your marginal tax rate. If the project doesn't generate its projected returns, you will be out of pocket after tax.

♀ TIP

I am a big fan of the famous Nike advertising campaign. When you get great advice then 'Just Do It'. I get really annoyed when my clients don't follow through because they forgot or were too lazy to get around to it.

Thank you for taking the time to read this book. I hope it has been of benefit to you. Over time, I have no doubt that these strategies will save you significant amounts of money—and during tough times, every single dollar counts!

👍 TAX FACT

As mentioned in the introduction, not every single tip outlined in this book is applicable to everyone. But I guarantee you that at least one of these tips will save you more than the cost of this book. In fact, the purchase of this book as reference material for your tax affairs will be tax-deductible. Do you still have that receipt?

You will be surprised how many slackos there are that miss out on easy money despite how simple some of these strategies are. Take the superannuation co-contribution, for example.

If you procrastinated every year since the introduction of super co-contribution in 2003 (and there are a lot of people out there who have) and kept on forgetting to contribute post-tax dollars into super, you have missed out on potentially $15 500 of free money from the government. With savings generally doubling every ten years, your retirement savings could be almost $31 000 higher as well.

♀ TIP

The simplest way to remind yourself to action something is to put a follow-up reminder in your calendar. If you have a computer with an online calendar, such as the one in Microsoft Outlook, you can set up reminders on a regular basis as 'new appointments'. When the reminder pops up on your screen in the future, don't 'dismiss' until you have actioned it. Press 'snooze' instead.

Research has found that 100 per cent of action plans that are not started result in the goals set out in the action plans not being achieved.

Can you and your family afford to miss out on this amount of money simply by leaving things to next week or next year?

I wish you and your family much happiness and hope that life is not too taxing!

GLOSSARY

$1000 upfront tax concession: If you acquire ESS interests under a taxed-upfront scheme that meets certain conditions, you will be eligible to receive a tax concession of up to $1000 if your taxable income after adjustments is $180 000 or less.

30-day rule: If you dispose of your ESS interest within 30 days after the deferred taxing point, the deferred taxing point becomes the date of that disposal.

45-day rule: See *holding period rule*.

ABN: Australian Business Number; a unique identifying number issued to all entities registered in the Australian Business Register.

ABR: Australian Business Register; the extensive database of identity information provided by businesses when they register for an ABN www.abr.gov.au.

ACCC: Australian Competition and Consumer Commission; government organisation responsible for ensuring compliance with the *Trade Practices Act 1974* www.accc.gov.au.

accruals basis: If you account for an invoice but do not receive the cash, you are using an accruals basis of accounting; you can use the cash basis if your annual turnover is $1 million or less.

adjusted taxable income: The sum of:

* taxable income
* reportable fringe benefits
* reportable superannuation contributions
* total net investment loss.

allowable deduction: An expense you can deduct from your assessable income.

APRA: Australian Prudential Regulation Authority—APRA is responsible for regulating certain types of super funds www.apra.gov.au.

ASIC: Australian Securities & Investments Commission—the corporate, markets and financial services regulator in Australia www.asic.gov.au.

assessable income: The income you derive, before deducting allowable deductions, that is liable to tax.

associate: Associates include people and entities closely associated with you, such as relatives, or closely connected companies or trustees of a trust (other than the trustee of an employee share trust). For example, a partner in a partnership is an associate of the partnership and an individual's spouse is an associate of the individual. You may also be an associate of a self managed super fund in which you are a member or a family trust of which you are a beneficiary.

ASX: Australian Securities Exchange—the marketplace for trading shares, bonds and other securities in Australia www.asx.com.au.

ATO: Australian Taxation Office—the ATO's role is to manage and collect tax as well as act as regulator of self managed super funds in Australia www.ato.gov.au.

AUSTRAC: Australian Transaction Reports and Analysis Centre—Australia's anti–money laundering and counter-terrorism financing regulator and specialist financial intelligence unit www.austrac.gov.au.

BAS: Business activity statement—a statement under the pay-as-you-go system that you prepare at the end of each quarter to remit GST, PAYG withholding and PAYG instalments.

beneficiary: A person who is potentially entitled to a payment from a trust.

bitcoin: The first and most popular decentralised cryptocurrency and worldwide payment system which works without a central bank or single administrator.

blockchain: A continuously growing list of records, called blocks, which are linked and secured using cryptography, the public transaction ledger for the cryptocurrency bitcoin.

bonus shares: Free shares issued by a company usually in proportion to your current share holdings.

brokerage fee: The fee charged by a stockbroker when you buy or sell shares.

business real property: A property that is used wholly or exclusively by one or more businesses.

buy contract note: An invoice you receive from a stockbroker at the time you buy shares. It will summarise the details of the transaction and can be used to calculate a capital gain or capital loss for taxation purposes.

CAANZ: Institute of Chartered Accountants in Australia and New Zealand—one of the three professionally recognised accounting bodies in Australia (along with CPA Australia and IPA) www.charteredaccountantsanz.com.

call option: The right, but not the obligation, to buy the underlying shares at an agreed price on or before the date of expiration.

capital expenditure: Money spent on assets such as plant and equipment, goodwill, buildings, patents and copyrights.

capital loss: The loss you incur when you sell CGT assets such as shares for a price that's below their reduced cost base; under Australian tax law a capital loss can only be offset against a capital gain.

capital protection loan: A loan to buy shares where you can protect yourself from incurring a loss if your share portfolio falls in value.

cash basis: If you issue (or receive) an invoice but do not account for the sale (or purchase) until the cash is received (or paid), you are using a cash basis of accounting; you can use the cash basis if your annual turnover is $1 million or less.

CCB: Child care benefit—government benefit that helps eligible families with the cost of child care.

cents per kilometre method: One of the two methods of claiming a deduction for car expenses. You can use this method up to a maximum of 5000 business kilometres at a flat rate of 68 cents per kilometre from the 2018–19 income year.

CGT: Capital gains tax—the tax payable on the disposal of an investment asset that was acquired after 19 September 1985. It is not a separate tax, just part of your income tax. The most common way you make a capital gain (or capital loss) is by selling or disposing of assets such as real estate, shares or managed fund investments.

CGT asset register: A register you keep to record all CGT assets you own, such as your share portfolio.

CGT event: Normally arises when there's a change in ownership of a CGT asset.

company: A separate legal entity, registered by ASIC, that can carry on a business in its own name; a company raises capital through the issue of shares.

company tax rate: 27.5 per cent of a small company's taxable income (30 per cent for companies with aggregated annual turnover greater than $50 million).

complying super fund: A super fund that is regulated by the ATO and has been issued with a notice of compliance; complying funds that meet the *SIS Act 1993* standards qualify for a concessional tax rate.

concessional tax rate: Super funds that comply with the SIS Act 1993 qualify for the concessional tax rate of 15 per cent; non-complying super funds do not receive the concessional tax rate and are taxed at 45 per cent. Contributions made by individuals earning more than $250 000 are taxed at 30 per cent.

condition of release: A condition, normally retirement, that must be satisfied before you can access your benefits in a superannuation fund.

contribution: The money or asset directly contributed by an individual, an employer or another party into a super fund.

cost base: The cost base of an asset is generally what it costs you. It is made up of five elements:

- the money you paid or property you gave for the asset
- the incidental costs of acquiring or selling it (for example, brokerage and stamp duty)
- the costs of owning it (generally this will not apply to shares because you will usually have claimed or be entitled to claim these costs as tax deductions)
- the costs associated with increasing or preserving its value, or with installing or moving it
- the cost to you to preserve or defend your title or rights to it.

CPA Australia: One of the three professionally recognised accounting bodies in Australia (along with CAANZ and IPA) www.cpaaustralia.com.au.

CPI: Consumer price index—the general inflation index prepared by the Australian Bureau of Statistics that measures the change in the price of a fixed basket of goods bought by households.

cryptocurrency: A digital asset designed to work as a medium of exchange that uses cryptography to secure its transactions, to control the creation of additional units, and to verify the transfer of assets. Uses decentralised control through a blockchain, which is a public transaction database, functioning as a distributed ledger.

crystallise: To dispose of shares in order to create or realise a capital gain or capital loss.

dad and partner pay: Government benefit paid to the father of the newborn child (or partner of the birth parent) to help with costs after the birth of the baby. The pay is for up to two weeks at the minimum wage, and is taxable.

deferred taxing point: The earliest of the following times:

- seven years after you acquired a share/right
- the time you cease the employment in respect of which you acquired the share/right
- the time when there is no real risk of forfeiture and the scheme no longer genuinely restricts the disposal of the share/right.

dependants: People you look after who need your financial support; usually spouse and minor children.

depreciation: A non-cash expense which is the decline in value of an asset over time.

derived: Income you earn that is liable for tax.

DGR: Deductible gift recipient.

DICTO: Dependant (invalid and carer) tax offset— available to taxpayers who maintain a dependant who is genuinely unable to work due to carer obligation or disability. In this instance, eight dependency tax offsets have been consolidated into a single, streamlined and non-refundable offset.

DIDO: Drive-in drive-out—an arrangement where the employee drives a considerable distance from/to their normal residence to work for a number of days on a regular and rotational basis, and has a number of days off that are not the same days in consecutive weeks. Special LAFHA rules apply.

directors: Appointed by shareholders to manage and run the day-to-day operations of a company.

DisabilityCare Australia: The national disability insurance scheme funded by an increase in the Medicare levy (to 2 per cent) since 1 July 2014.

discounted capital gain: A 50 per cent reduction on the capital gain on disposal of CGT assets that were owned for at least 12 months.

discretionary trust: A trust where the trustee has discretion as to how the trust net income should be distributed to the beneficiaries.

dividend: A distribution of profit paid to shareholders of a company in proportion to the number of shares owned.

dividend reinvestment plan: A scheme where a company gives shareholders the option of reinvesting dividends in the form of new shares in the company, rather than receiving the dividends in cash.

Division 7A: A section of the Tax Act that contains anti-avoidance provisions which are aimed at preventing private company owners and their associates from avoiding dividend taxation by trying to access company profits in another form besides dividends.

Division 293 tax: A section of the Tax Act which reduces the tax concession on super contributions for individuals with income greater than the Division 293 threshold of $250 000 by increasing the superannuation tax rate from 15 to 30 per cent.

DIY super: Do-it-yourself superannuation, also known as an SMSF.

downsizer contributions: Contributions made by those aged 65 and over into superannuation within 90 days of sale of their home (of at least ten years) up to a maximum of $300 000 each. Excluded from the non-concessional contribution limit.

DRP: Dividend reinvestment plan.

election: When a taxpayer makes a choice, usually in writing, with respect to adopting a certain tax law ahead of another.

ESIC: Early stage innovation company. An unlisted Australian company with turnover less than $200 000 and expenses under $1 million in the preceding year plus satisfy one of two innovations tests. Special tax incentives are available to its sophisticated investors.

ESS: Employee share scheme; a scheme under which shares, stapled securities and rights (including options) to acquire shares and stapled securities in a company are provided to its employees (including current, past or prospective employees and their associates) in relation to their employment.

ESS interests: Shares, stapled securities, or rights (including options) to acquire shares or stapled securities.

ESS statement: An annual statement that shows an estimate of any discounts you or your associates have received on your ESS interests.

ether: A popular cryptocurrency whose blockchain is generated by the Ethereum platform.

ETP: Employment termination payment (previously known as an eligible termination payment); a lump-sum payment made due to your employment being terminated.

Export Market Development Grant: A scheme that provides grants up to $150 000 to small and medium-sized businesses who incur eligible export promotion expenses. Administered by Austrade.

family discretionary trust: A trust whose membership is ordinarily made up of family beneficiaries; the trustee has discretion to distribute trust net income to certain beneficiaries.

FBT: Fringe benefits tax.

FIFO: Fly-in fly-out—an arrangement where the employee flies from/to their normal residence to work for a number of days on a regular and rotational basis and has a number of days off that are not the same days in consecutive weeks. Special LAFHA rules apply.

financial year: The period from 1 July to 30 June the following year.

foreign tax credit: Foreign tax paid on income derived from overseas sources that can be offset against Australian tax payable on taxable income derived from worldwide sources.

franked dividends: Dividends paid by an Australian resident company from profits that have had Australian company tax paid on them.

franking credits: The amounts of tax paid previously by a company that are allocated to dividends paid to shareholders; the taxpayer receives the credits in their income tax assessment to avoid double taxation; also known as imputation credits.

GIC: General interest charge—interest rate imposed by the ATO for late payment of tax.

GST: Goods and services tax—10 per cent tax on goods and services.

HELP: Higher Education Loan Program.

holding period rule: The rule where shareholders must continuously hold shares 'at risk' for at least 45 days (90 days for preference shares) around the ex-dividend date in order to be eligible for the franking tax offset. However, under the small shareholder exemption, this rule does not apply if your total franking credit entitlement is below $5000, which is roughly equivalent to receiving a fully franked dividend of $11 666 (based on the current tax rate of 30 per cent for companies).

IAS: Instalment activity statement—a statement under the pay-as-you-go system that you prepare at the end of each reporting period disclosing certain income that is liable to tax.

imputation credit: See *franking credits*.

income tax: A federal tax that you pay on taxable income you derive.

income tax return: An annual form lodged with the ATO disclosing your taxable income.

incurred: The point in time when you can legally claim a deduction, usually when you have a commitment and a legal obligation to make a payment for certain goods and services you receive.

indeterminate right: A right to acquire at a future time either:

- shares or cash (at the discretion of your employer)
- a number of shares, where that number cannot be determined at the time of acquisition of the right but will be determined at a later time.

initial repairs: Costs to rectify damage, defects or deterioration that existed at the time of purchasing a property and considered to be capital in nature and not deductible for tax purposes.

instalment warrant: A form of derivative or financial product that entails borrowing to invest in an underlying asset, such as a share or real property, with limited risk to the investor. The underlying asset is held in trust during the life of the loan to provide limited security for the lender. The investor is required to pay one or more future instalments to the lender.

investment strategy: A document setting out how you intend to invest your benefits in an SMSF; it must be in writing and must consider investment risks, the likely returns and whether you have sufficient cash on hand to discharge liabilities when they fall due.

IP: Intellectual property.

IPA: IPA Institute of Public Accountants, formerly National Institute of Accountants—one of the three professionally recognised accounting bodies in Australia (along with CAANZ and CPA Australia) www.publicaccountants.org.au.

ITAA 1936: *The Income Tax Assessment Act 1936.*

ITAA 1997: *The Income Tax Assessment Act 1997.*

LAFHA: Living-away-from-home allowance—a tax-free allowance paid to employees who are required to perform their work duties away from their usual place of residence.

litecoin: A cryptocurrency that uses Scrypt as a hashing algorithm.

LITO: Low-income tax offset.

LMITO: Low and middle income tax offset.

LMR: Lost members register—a register maintained by the ATO showing a list of lost and unclaimed super.

low-income tax offset: A general tax offset you can claim if your taxable income is below a certain threshold; the tax offset is reduced by 1.5 cents for every dollar you earn above the threshold. Taxpayers who receive this offset are also entitled to the low to middle income tax offset.

low and middle income tax offset: A general tax offset in addition to the low-income tax offset that you can claim if your taxable income is below a certain threshold; the tax offset is reduced by 1.5 cents for every dollar you earn above the threshold.

low-value pool: A pool of depreciable assets, each with a written-down value under $1000, which can be depreciated at a more favourable pool rate of 37.5 per cent per annum.

margin call: The shortfall required if the value of your shares, funded by a margin loan, falls below a certain level.

margin loan: A form of borrowing to fund a share portfolio.

marginal tax rate: The rate of tax applicable to the last dollar of your taxable income; your average tax rate on your entire taxable income is generally lower than your marginal tax rate.

Medicare levy: A 2 per cent levy charged on your taxable income.

Medicare levy surcharge: An extra levy (up to 1.5 per cent) charged on taxable income when taxpayers do not have private health insurance and their 'adjusted taxable income' is above a certain amount.

MyDeductions: An ATO-developed app that you can download onto a mobile device to make it easier and more convenient to keep your tax deductions and income records all in one place. Syncs in with MyTax at financial year end.

MyTax: The ATO's online tax preparation program for self-preparers with simple tax affairs www.ato.gov.au/MyTax.

NDIS (National Disability Insurance Scheme): Tax-exempt assistance received by eligible people with a disability www.ndis.gov.au

negative gearing: Occurs when the net rental income from an investment property, after deducting other expenses, is less than the interest on the borrowings, a very popular tax strategy employed by Australians; these properties are purchased with the assistance of borrowed funds and partly repaid by the tax benefits subsequently received.

non-complying super fund: A super fund that is not residing in Australia or that has been issued with a notice of non-compliance because it does not comply with the *SIS Act 1993;* non-complying super funds do not receive the concessional tax rate and are taxed at 45 per cent.

non-resident: A person who does not normally reside in Australia and has no intention of living here; a non-resident is liable to pay tax only on income sourced in Australia. People who are temporarily in Australia for a working holiday are treated as non-residents for tax purposes, regardless of how long they are here.

notice of compliance: The ATO will issue this notice if it makes a determination that a fund complies with the *SIS Act 1993;* the determination is only made after an SMSF annual return has been lodged with the ATO.

objection: A formal challenge against an ATO assessment or decision.

option: An option is a form of right: if you receive an option, you make an agreement with the provider of the option, allowing you to buy shares or stapled securities during a certain time period, for a particular price (the exercise price); you then have the right, but not the obligation, to exercise the option.

paid parental leave: A government benefit paid to a parent of a newborn child to help care for the baby; the pay is for up to 18 weeks at the minimum wage and is taxable.

partnership: Two or more people in business with a common view to making a profit.

PAYG (pay-as-you-go) withholding: The tax deducted from an employee's wages by an employer and remitted to the ATO.

PAYG withholding variation application: A form, which is virtually a mini tax return, that estimates your taxable income for the upcoming year to reduce the tax deducted from your pay packet.

pension age: The age used to determine eligibility for certain government benefits, including the age pension; the pension age is currently 65.5, rising to 66 from 1 July 2019 and increasing to 67 by 2023.

positive gearing: The opposite of negative gearing; it occurs when the net rental income from an investment property, after deducting other expenses, is greater than the interest on the borrowings.

preservation age: The minimum age at which a member can access their preserved benefits; a benefit may be paid earlier if the member has met a condition of release; the preservation age varies depending on when the member was born.

preserved benefits: The superannuation fund benefits that you can access when you reach your preservation age and retire.

private ruling: Written advice you receive from the ATO about how it would interpret the tax laws in respect of a specific issue you raise.

PSI: Personal services income — business income that is principally derived via the personal exertion of an individual and is subject to certain tests in order to be assessable in a company or trust.

put option: The right, not the obligation, to sell underlying shares at an agreed price on or before the expiry date; a form of insurance in a falling market.

quantity surveyor: A professional within the construction industry who is recognised by the ATO to have the appropriate construction costing skills to calculate the cost of items for the purposes of tax depreciation schedules.

reduced cost base: The cost base of a CGT asset minus certain expenditure that has been allowed as a tax deduction; used to calculate a capital loss.

registered tax agent: A person who is authorised to give you advice in respect of managing your tax affairs and can lodge a tax return on your behalf; the fee they charge for their services is ordinarily a tax-deductible expense.

reportable fringe benefits: The grossed-up taxable value of certain fringe benefits provided to you on your payment summary.

reportable superannuation contributions: The sum of any contributions that you make to your superannuation fund for which you can claim a deduction in the financial year under Subdivision 290-C of the *Income Tax Assessment Act 1997*, and the contributions your employer makes for you

resident: A person who normally resides in Australia; taxed on their worldwide income at the marginal tax rates.

Restart wage subsidy: A program that pays employers up to $10 000 (GST inclusive) over 6 months who employ and retain eligible job seekers who are 50 years of age or older, and who have been unemployed and on income support for six months or more.

rights issue: The right to buy additional shares direct from the company at a specified price (usually below market price) on a specified future date; usually linked to the number of shares you hold.

salary sacrifice: A strategy where you ask your employer to put an additional amount of your pre-tax salary into super.

self-assessment: The tax system in Australia where the onus is on you to declare to the ATO the correct amount of income you derive each year and claim the correct amount of tax deductions.

sell contract note: The invoice you receive from a stockbroker at the time you sell your shares; it will summarise the details of the transaction and can be used to calculate a capital gain or capital loss for taxation purposes.

senior Australian: Anyone aged over 65.

senior and pensioner tax offset (SAPTO): An effective tax-free threshold for eligible senior Australians of $32 279 for singles and $28 974 each for couples.

SFSS: Student financial supplement scheme — a voluntary loan scheme to help tertiary students cover their expenses while studying.

SG: Superannuation guarantee—compulsory super contributions paid every quarter by employers at a minimum of 9.50 per cent of employees' ordinary time earnings. Gradually increasing to 12 per cent by 2025–26.

shareholder: A person who owns shares in a company.

share investor: A person who invests in the sharemarket with the predominant purpose of deriving dividends and long-term capital growth.

share trader: A person who is carrying on a business trading in shares with the predominant purpose of making a profit.

sharing economy: A mode of consumption whereby goods and services are not owned by a single user, but rather only temporarily accessed by members of a network and underutilised assets are shared, either for free or for a fee. Also known as the access economy, peer-to-peer (P2P) economy, or collaborative economy it includes Uber, AirbnB, Camplify, Menulog, Airtasker, Fiverr and Freelancer.

SIS: *Superannuation Industry (Supervision) Act 1993.*

SMSF: Self managed superannuation fund, also known as DIY super; a super fund that you manage yourself.

sophisticated investor: An investor as defined under Corporations Law who has a gross income of at least $250 000 in each of the two preceding years; net assets over $2 500 000; and/or controls at least $10 million of gross assets.

statutory method: A method used to calculate FBT on company cars based on the total number of kilometres travelled and applying a statutory fraction to the cost of the car provided. See table 2.2 on p. 56.

super co-contribution: If you make personal contributions to your super and are otherwise eligible, the Federal Government will help boost your account with a super co-contribution of up to $500 per financial year; the amount of the co-contribution will depend on your total income level (you can earn less than $53 564) and the amount of personal contributions you make.

superannuation fund: A fund set up to finance retirement; benefits normally cannot be accessed until you reach your preservation age and retire from the workforce.

tax: Something we all hate paying and love to try and minimise...legally!

taxable income: The amount of income that's liable to tax; taxable income equals assessable income less allowable deductions.

tax-deferred scheme: Employee share schemes that allow you to defer paying tax; generally, you will pay tax on the discount you receive when you acquire ESS interests in the financial year in which you acquired them; however, in certain circumstances, you may defer paying the tax for a period of up to seven years.

tax-free threshold: The lowest tax bracket ($18 200) at which an Australian resident pays no tax; non-residents (including those on working holidays in Australia) cannot claim the tax-free threshold.

tax man: The nickname affectionately given to the Commissioner of Taxation and/or the Australian Taxation Office in general.

tax offset: A tax credit or rebate that you can use to reduce the amount of tax payable on taxable income you derive.

tax refund: Something we all love to get from the tax man each year.

tax ruling: A public ruling issued by the ATO to explain and clarify how the Taxation Commissioner interprets tax legislation in respect of a specific issue.

TFN: Tax file number — a unique number issued by the ATO to individuals and organisations to increase the efficiency in administering tax and other Federal Government systems.

TFN withholding: Tax withheld at the highest marginal rate (47 per cent) on unfranked dividends and bank interest if you have not quoted your TFN; taxpayers need to include the amounts withheld in their tax return in order to receive the credit in their assessment.

total net investment loss: The sum for the financial year of the amount by which the individual's:

* deductions from financial investments are greater than their income from those investments
* rental property deductions are greater than their rental property income.

Trade Support Loan: A loan paid in instalments totalling up to $20 000 over four years to assist eligible apprentices with everyday costs while they complete their apprenticeship www .australianapprenticeships.gov.au.

trust: A legal obligation binding a person (the trustee) who has control over the investment assets (for instance, a share portfolio) for the benefit of beneficiaries.

trustee: The individual or entity that has the responsibility of ensuring that the trust or super fund is operated in accordance with its trust deed; trustees must also comply with relevant legislation and regulations.

TtR: Transition to retirement—strategy available to those aged over 57 to access up to 10 per cent of their super each year to supplement their income.

under a legal disability: A beneficiary of a trust, such as a minor, a bankrupt or an insane person, who is not in a legal position to deal with a trust distribution.

unfranked dividends: Dividends paid by an Australian resident company from profits that have not had Australian company tax paid on them.

warrant: An option issued that gives the holder the right, but not the obligation, to buy from the issuer or sell to the issuer underlying shares at an agreed price on or before the expiry date.

wash sale: Selling shares to predominantly make a capital loss and gain a tax benefit, then buying the shares back immediately.

working holiday maker: A backpacker temporarily visiting Australia under visa subclass 417 (working holiday) or 462 (work and holiday). Pays 15 per cent on the first $37 000 of income earned and normal resident tax rates thereafter.

BIBLIOGRAPHY

A New Tax System (Goods and Services Tax) Act 1999.

A New Tax System (Goods and Services Tax) Regulations 1999.

Arnold, BR, Bateman, H, Ferguson A and Raftery AM 2015, *The size, cost and asset allocation of Australian self-managed superannuation funds*, Centre for International Finance and Regulation, working paper.

Australian Bureau of Statistics 2019, 5206.0 Australian National Accounts: National Income, Expenditure and Product: Table 1.

Australian Prudential Regulation Authority 2019a, Monthly Banking Statistics—December 2018.

Australian Prudential Regulation Authority 2019b, Quarterly Superannuation Performance—December 2018.

Australian Securities Exchange 2017, 2017 Australian Investor Study.

Australian Securities Exchange 2019, Historical market statistics—December 2018.

Australian Taxation Office 2019, Self-managed super fund statistical report—December 2018.

Barkoczy, S 2019, *Core Tax Legislation & Study Guide,* 22nd edn, CCH Australia, Sydney.

Bird, R, Foster, FD, Gray, J, Raftery, AM, Thorp, S, Yeung, D 2018, *Who starts a self-managed superannuation fund and why?* Australian Journal of Management, Vol 43, Issue 3, pp. 373-403.

CCH Australia 2019, *Australian GST Legislation with Overview,* 22nd edn, CCH Australia, Sydney.

CCH Australia 2019, *Australian Master Tax Guide,* 64th edn, CCH Australia, Sydney.

Fringe Benefits Tax Assessment Act 1986.

Income Tax Assessment Act 1936.

Income Tax Assessment Act 1997.

Income Tax Assessment Regulations 1997.

Income Tax Regulations 1936.

Pinto, D, Kendall, K and Sadiq, K 2019, *Fundamental Tax Legislation,* 6th edn, Thomson, Sydney.

Raftery, AM 2014, The size, cost, asset allocation and audit attributes of Australian self-managed superannuation funds, thesis.

Woellner, R, Barkoczy, S, Murphy, S, Evans, C and Pinto, D 2019, *Australian Taxation Law,* 29th edn, CCH Australia Limited, Sydney.

INDEX

For an explanation of technical terms refer to the Glossary on pages 251–266.

9 780730 371472